HOW TO BE A
QUICK TURN REAL ESTATE
ENTREPRENEUR
IN ANY
ECONOMY

RON LEGRAND®

Table of Contents

How To Be A Quick Turn Real Estate Entrepreneur In Any Economy

Dedication

There are so many good people in my life to dedicate this book to. I couldn't decide who should be on that list so I'm dedicating it to the one who deserves it the most... YOU. It's all about you the reader, the one who's looking for answers about how to create financial freedom and get your life back.

You're the hero here. A true American struggling to get the most out of this short life you can. You're who gave me my wealth and the one I've dedicated my life to serve and hopefully you become one of those I can add to my growing League of Extraordinary Real Estate Millionaires.

It's my hope I say something here that stimulates you to take action now. It's only a marginal shift from a life of mediocrity to the life of your dreams. Small actions constantly implemented with dogged determination to win and a conviction to let no SOB steal your dreams. I dedicate this book to your success and expect you to share it with people you like.

Read it once or twice and make your decision to put it to good use. It won't do a thing for you on the shelf.

I hope to see you one day soon at one of our live events. There is plenty of information in the back for your review. When I do see you, be sure to bring your spouse or loved one. I love to see families grow together and share their new lifestyle with others.

Yes, you are my hero.

Who Is Ron LeGrand®?

When I first got involved with real estate, I was a dead broke auto mechanic trying to make enough money to make ends meet. There was no such thing as disposable income around my house. It was all disposed of before I got it. Thirty-five-years-old and bankrupt. I didn't have a clue what I wanted to be when I grew up; but I knew it wasn't fixing cars in the hot Florida sun.

The year was 1982. I saw an ad that said something like "Come learn how to buy real estate with no money or credit and get rich by next Thursday." That appealed to me because I had no money or credit and I kinda liked the rich idea. So I attended the free seminar.

The instructor got us all excited about real estate and showed us how people were buying real estate with no money down. Then he said that if you pay $450 and attend our two-day training this weekend, we'll show you all the secrets. I wanted in, but I had a big problem—actually 450 big problems.

But something compelled me to find a way to get the money, and that's what I did. I borrowed it from two friends and showed up for the seminar. That decision changed my life forever, my family's life and their family's lives for generations to come, not to mention hundreds of thousands of my students and their descendants into the millions. That one small split-second decision that could have gone either way made me millions of dollars and spawned countless numbers of millionaires all over North America and in countries I can't even pronounce.

In fact, most of the stuff taught in that seminar was over my head. I was clueless and could barely spell real estate. But I picked up one idea I felt I could use, and within three weeks I made my first $3,000 from real estate using no money or credit, as I had none of either. I immediately called my boss and said, "I'm upping my income . . . see you around!"

The biggest thing that seminar did was get me involved in real estate and committed to changing my lifestyle. For years I'd been looking for something but didn't know what it was. When I got my hands on that three grand, it became crystal clear that real estate was my future.

Fast-forward two years: I had amassed 276 units—some single-family, some apartments—not including some I sold along the way to live. I was a millionaire . . . on paper. I had over $1 million in equity two years after starting with no money or credit.

Reality Arrives!

I sat down one Friday evening to pay my bills and realized my outgo was bigger than my income, and my upkeep was becoming my downfall. All I had accomplished was creating a big, ugly mess. I'd spent two years buying the wrong properties the wrong way in the wrong areas for the wrong reasons. I built my empire on a house of cards, not on a solid foundation.

You see, I really didn't understand the real estate business. I just bought properties because I could without money or credit. I bought all the crap savvy investors wouldn't touch. They'd already been to the school I was about to graduate from—"The School of Hard Knocks." All my low-income properties in war zone areas with brainless tenants were sucking me dry, financially and mentally. My days were spent solving these tenants' petty problems and listening to all the worthless reasons why they couldn't pay rent.

I spent the next five years selling off my junk for dimes on the dollar. It took me seven years in the business to really understand it and get my life back. Oh, I made a good living during that time—several times my previous income—but I sure wish I'd have known myself back then and had the system that my students have now. On second thought, it wouldn't have mattered anyway. I wouldn't have listened. I'm a man, and men don't follow instructions. It's the way we're wired.

After about seven years in the business and over 400 houses later, I built an easy system to turn real estate into cash immediately, cash monthly, and cash later. I made it a real business anyone could operate from home to make obscene amounts of money.

That's about the time I started teaching what I had learned. Somewhere along the line someone called me *"The World's Leading Expert at Quick Turning Houses"* and the name stuck.

In the late 1990s the information company I built went public with revenues exceeding $20 million annually from my books, tapes, and seminars.

Now fast-forward a few more years of teaching what I know while simultaneously doing what I teach, and I will admit I'm a weird dude. I've bought and sold over 3,000 houses and still do 2 or 3 a month with an average profit over $40,000 with the help of my executive assistant, who spends 5 to 10 hours a week at real estate.

Over the years I've created a mountain of home study products, written millions of words in print, and shared the platform with past presidents, movie stars, actors, politicians, sports heroes, business leaders, super-wealthy individuals from all professions, and some of the best speakers in the world. I've spoken to audiences as small as 20 and as large as 20,000 in hotel meeting rooms and coliseums all across North America.

I've gazed in amazement and sheer joy as so many thousands of my clients and new friends have pulled themselves out of financial mediocrity, or downright poverty, and made themselves financially independent millionaires and some even multimillionaires from the words that left my lips and the time we spent together.

So many of these new millionaires have now become leaders reaching out a hand to those in need to help them climb the ladder to success. My legacy has spread like a swarm of locusts, and millions will be affected or already have been by the positive impact I made with a few carefully chosen words that left my lips or got put in print at a time when students were ready to receive them and convert them to action. New generations will profit directly or indirectly from the words in this book because they attended one of my seminars, then used the information and passed it on. *When the student is ready, the teacher will appear.*

Much of my time now is spent in front of good people who are serious about getting rich and will do what it takes to become one of the 3 percent who can not only say but prove they have achieved true wealth.

People constantly ask me why I continue to teach. It's hard for them to understand why a multimillionaire would take the time to work with those who aren't.

My answer is simple, really. First, make no mistake about it; I get paid well for teaching. It's not a mercy mission, and we're not a non-profit organization. Second, I have to do something with my time; golf, fishing, and diving get old quickly. Making millionaires never gets old, and I can't think of anything I'd rather do in my life. It's fun to be me, and I love doing it.

Besides, I've been married about 50 years to one woman. Her name is Beverly and between the "Honey, do's" (her requests) and the nine grandchildren (three live on our estate), it's nice to get away once in a while. Beverly says that even though we've been married 50 years, it's closer to 3 if you take out my travel time.

Truthfully, I'm just a simple auto mechanic with a redneck background who barely got out of high school. I'd rather have a good hamburger than a steak. I hate wine and all other alcoholic beverages. I smoke cigars, listen to country music and jazz, and go to the movies a lot. We have horses, cats, a dog, and chickens; we grow stuff in our own garden and, yes, I even have my very own tractor I use to plow that garden.

So there you have it—the real me. Now let's spend the rest of this book on you and how I can add your name to our millionaires club . . . quickly.

Part One

Why Real Estate?

Chapter 1
You Can Get A Big Check In Days, Not Years

I started in the real estate investment business after attending a two—day seminar back in 1982. Luckily, one or two things I learned there worked. I quickly discovered a whole new world of opportunity was out there that I'd never been exposed to—a world built around using my brain, not my back, with huge paydays and freedom from swapping hours for dollars.

Not long after that seminar, I had 276 rental units. That may sound wonderful, but I sat down to pay the family utility bills one day and discovered there wasn't enough money to cover them, which led me to take a hard look at how I had been operating. I had become a paper millionaire quickly. It had been easy to accumulate equity, but I had no cash. I couldn't eat equity or pay bills with it. That's when I started to look for cash flow. It was this chain of events that led me to develop the quick turn method to generate fast cash.

You can make $10,000 to $100,000 or more in this business with just one deal, even in a low-priced market. It doesn't take many deals like that each year to make a good living. This book is full of real-life examples of people who have reclaimed their lives after I showed them the magical world of quick turn real estate.

Most people work all their lives to get pensions equal to half the wages they were earning—wages that didn't even cover their bills. You have the opportunity to take the future in your own hands and build cash flow that will continue whether you have a job or not.

The first step is to take care of today's cash flow needs before you start building your empire. Once those needs are met and you possess the ability to generate cash, there are countless ways to turn the cash into a consistent flow and provide for a secure retirement.

➢ *You Don't Have To Wait*

Some people think the only way to make money in real estate is to buy a rental property, sit on it for 20 or 30 years, contend with bad tenants, plugged toilets, and negative cash flow, and then sell for a profit. But, that assumes there is something left of the house and that inflation hasn't decreased the property's value. It also assumes that during the holding period the owners don't get so frustrated with the property management they just quit, which is what happens to many people.

My intention is not to discourage the use of real estate as a retirement tool or to indicate that people shouldn't hold property for the long term. In fact, I honestly believe the greatest profits take time to develop. Huge fortunes have been amassed (some accidentally, it must be admitted) by the people who sat on a property for a long time, then awoke one day to find the value increased by 10 or 20 times the purchase price.

But, most people don't have the luxury of time or the blind luck to make money while they sleep. And most are not properly equipped with knowledge and a clear-cut action plan before they start to buy properties. I've seen many people who think owning a few houses will make them rich enough in five years to retire and go fishing all day. More often, the opposite happens. The houses drag down the owners who weren't properly trained to deal with the realities of real estate ownership. Those owners didn't have the knowledge you'll get from this book—knowledge that will keep you in control.

➢ *The Good News*

If your intentions are to buy real estate to generate more cash, and if you want to have the cash now rather than years from now, listen up. There is a way to do just that. It involves flipping houses fast, or what I call "quick turning."

I have bought and sold more than 3,000 houses for fast cash profit. Along the way, I developed a system that anyone who has the desire and willingness to learn can duplicate and make work for them, regardless of their financial condition. We're going to study all the aspects of this system, step-by-step, in the following chapters.

If you think you need a lot of money and good credit or you have to be a genius to make money in real estate—it just isn't so! In this book, you'll learn how to convert houses to fast cash, no matter where in North America you live, and regardless of whether you're wealthy or flat broke. In fact, if you're broke, you may actually have an advantage, because you have no choice but to *learn* before you leap. Those who have money tend to leap before they learn, then blame their failure on the system, the economy, their spouses, and their mothers-in-law—everyone except themselves. In this or any other business you have to learn the fundamentals before leaping.

These are the three basic reasons to by non-owner-occupied real estate:

- ♦ **Quick cash profits**
- ♦ **Monthly cash flow**
- ♦ **Long-term growth**

"But wait," you say, "what about tax shelters?" Forget tax shelters! Those days are gone. Many properties bought for tax shelters before the 1986 tax change were soon owned by the Resolution Trust Corporation (RTC) or the lending institution. This is especially true for such large properties as apartment and commercial buildings that were sold for a fraction of their former value. Today, tax benefits are a bonus, not a reason to buy.

Once you're sure your family's needs are being met, you can afford to invest in some "keepers" for long-term growth. You'll learn more about that strategy in the following chapters. For now, I'll assume you want to know how to make fast cash without using your money or credit.

➤ *Why Real Estate?*

One thing is sure: People always need a place to live!

Why not be in a business that will never lack customers? Why not work at something that produces paychecks in the thousands, whether you are involved part-time or full-time? How would you like to go where you want, when you want, stay as long as you want, and never worry about what's happening while you're away? And then there's the recognition you'll get for being a person who can find houses for people who never thought they could be homeowners.

Best of all, why not be in a business that's recession proof? You'll learn how to make money with real estate in spite of the economy, interest rates, or the market situation. The only real difference between the "haves" and the "have-nots" is knowledge converted to action.

When I started in 1982, the prime rate was 18 percent. Times were tough. Money was tight and chaos rampant in the real estate industry. Realtors® were dropping like flies, and Wall Street had no kind words for real estate.

Yet somehow I managed to buy 23 properties my first six months in business without using a dime of my own money and made an average profit on each deal of $17,000 per house. Me . . . a dead broke auto mechanic with no previous real estate experience and a bankruptcy on my record. Even though I was new and clueless, I managed to make more money in my *first* six months than I had made the previous year swapping hours for dollars 60 hours a week.

Today my experience is quite normal for thousands of my students who exceed their job income quickly with real estate. You'll read about a few in the following chapters. It didn't take me long to learn that *wealth comes from chaos*, and when everyone else is complaining how tough times are, smart people smell opportunity and find a way to capitalize.

➢ *Little Or No Money Or Credit Needed*

There are two ways to lose in my world. One, write a big check to buy a house; don't write a big check and you can't lose a big check. It isn't rocket science. You can buy all the houses you need, including your own primary residence, without spending a dime of your own money. You'll see a preponderance of evidence of that in this book.

Second, you lose in my world by guaranteeing debt. We don't apply for loans, fill out an application, and suck up to bankers in my world. Your credit won't be needed; if you use it, you're doing business incorrectly and setting yourself up for a fall. Stay out of banks—I'll show you how my students and I are buying millions of dollars in real estate with no personal liability. If you insist on breaking this rule, I can promise you your empire will be built on a house of cards, not on a solid foundation.

There's actually a third way you can add to this list of ways to lose in real estate one of equal importance to the first two. That way can be avoided, however, by following a rule that will make the difference between whether you love this business or hate it:

Don't make promises you can't keep.

If you don't lie to the people you deal with and simply tell it like it is . . . you won't have to remember who you lied to last. What an amazing idea. We simply deal with those who want to deal with us and forget the rest. More on that later...

➢ It Works Everywhere

Where there are people who live in houses, there are people who want to sell houses and others who want to buy, regardless of the economic climate or geographic location. It was that way before you were born, and it'll be that way after you're gone.

I tell my students that if it doesn't work where you live, you can always move. But as soon as you're out of town, it'll start working for everyone else. If *you* say it won't work, it never will. I believe the best place to do a deal is in your own backyard. If you can't do deals where you live, moving won't help. Only training can fix the problem—not a U-Haul truck.

➢ Every Day's A Pleasure To Go To Work

When I was a mechanic, I hated to go to work. I went because I thought I had to. Groceries were a requirement around my house. I'd work 12-hour days and come home with burnt hands, greasy fingernails, and a lousy attitude.

Then I got into real estate. I couldn't wait to go to work. Every day was exciting. I was in charge, and on fire with passion for my work.

As a mechanic, weekends and vacations were what I lived for. As my own boss, I didn't want to quit on weekends; I wanted to work. To this day I take vacations because my wife says we should. Personally, I'd prefer a postcard, but when you've been married as long as I have, you learn to do what you're told. We've been married for nearly 40 years, and she's still putting up with me. Four children and nine grandchildren later, here's the secret to marriage that's worked for me!

You can be happy, or you can be right.

If I were you, gentlemen, I'd commit this to memory. It'll save you a lot of arguments.

As I write this, over 30 years after I got into real estate and over 3,000 houses later, and after training more than 500,000 students, doing hundreds of seminars, and creating a mountain of products . . . I still can't wait to get out of bed and go to work.

Some folks think that's the definition of a workaholic. I can assure you those folks are broke. You see, when you can't wait to get at what you love, even if it appears to be work to others, there's no such thing as stress in your life. Stress is for job slaves who hate what they do.

People without a mission don't understand missionaries.

➤ *Working From Home: No Large Investment Or Franchise Fee*

I worked from home for two years until Beverly, my wife, told me to get an office. Until recently I worked from an office outside my home where I did real estate and built other businesses. Today I'm back in my home with an outside office I visit occasionally to pester my COO, who runs our publishing business called Global Publishing, Inc.

Most of my students start working from home and just stay there. Many are making in excess of a million dollars a year from their home. Your biggest investment will be in your education. There you don't have a choice. There are only two ways to get a business education: the easy way and the hard way. As most of us do, I chose the hard way.

Obviously, the best way to learn any business is to follow a proven system and do no pioneering. I've made millionaires all over North America and other countries—people who chose to follow my system. Some did so immediately, whereas others tried it their way for a while and then came back to my way. Some tried it their way and were never seen again.

You get to decide whether you choose the easy way or the hard way. And remember this:
If you think education is expensive, try ignorance.

Fortunately, for you there's plenty of training available beyond this book. We have courses, live trainings on all aspects of quick turn real estate, and mentoring on the phone as well as seminars near where you live. The options are all on my Web site at **ronlegrand.com**.

➢ *A Part-Time Business That Produces A Full-Time Income*

Anyone spending more than 10 or 15 hours a week buying houses is wasting most of his or her time. I'll be the first to tell you that's exactly what most people do.

It's easy to be busy. It's more difficult to be productive. The real art is to be productive without being bushy. Do the right things and that's exactly what will happen to you. Do the wrong things and you'll feel like real estate is just another job sucking up all of your time.

People forget, or never learn, what business is supposed to be about. It should free up your time so you can enjoy life and do the things you can't do as a job slave. Business is supposed to provide for you and family and make life easier, not drag you into an endless vacuum of always being busy but never getting rich.

The most important lesson I ever learned in business is one of the toughest for most people to incorporate into their business and life, but doing it can make you filthy rich. By not doing it, your life will pass by in an endless parade of minutia. Here's the big lesson, my credo, and what has contributed to the success of so many of my millionaires:

The less I do, the more I make.

This is not about being busy. It's about making money—a lot of it. I'll suggest to you that the busier you become, the less you'll make.

Here's another wake–up call for you: If you can't do real estate part-time, you won't do any better at it full-time. More on this later...

"We are all self-made, but only the successful will admit it."

Earl Nightingale

Chapter 2
$10,000 A Month Technique

Here's a Technique Born from a Recession That Can Make You an Easy $10,000 a Month
by Ron LeGrand®

Over 25% of all the homes in America are over financed, some over 150% financed. This has resulted in millions of houses going into foreclosure and millions more headed there. It's also destroyed the financial status and credit of many good people.

But as usual, out of adversity comes opportunity and one of the biggest to come along in my 30 years is creating a revolution among home investors. Yours truly has created a new system, recorded it and built new agreements to match, and this technique has become the focus of my house business and more and more students who learn of it say the same.

The technique is called ACTS, Assignment of Contracts and Terms.

That means we get paid for assigning contracts, not buying houses we would have thrown away prior to ACTS, and every time we do we make a $5,000-$10,000 fee. Some are doing 6-8 a month, and you'll see why in a minute. Don't confuse this with wholesaling junkers. Here we're dealing with beautiful homes in great areas, and our only buyers are owner-occupants.

Let's start with the problem then your questions and my answers. When I'm done you should read this again because it will absolutely change your business model and probably double your cash flow. Here goes:

The Problems
- Over 50% of the FSBOs who call us, or we call are over leveraged, some 150% or more.
- Many FSBOs want more than their house is worth knowing their asking price is high but refuse to get a grip on reality and cannot be convinced it's overpriced.
- Some sellers are willing to create decent terms such as a lease-purchase or owner financing but not good enough

terms to make you want to close yourself and stay in the deal.

♦ Many sellers won't sell "subject-to" even when they're hurting.

♦ Some investors want immediate checks but don't want long-term deals such as lease-options or seller financing.

All these problems can go away with ACTS if the seller will work with you (and the majority will).

Let's start with an over leveraged example:
* ARV $200,000
* Loan $225,000
* Payment $1,450 PITI, 27 years left on mortgage.

The seller in this case has five choices:
1. Live in it until the equity returns through debt reduction and appreciation, which will take years. Some will, most won't, but remember they're trying to sell now or you wouldn't be talking with them.
2. They can walk away and let it go into foreclosure. Over five million have chosen this route and many more will. However many would rather find another solution.
3. They can hire a Realtor® and try a short sale. Some will but this means they must locate a Realtor® who will even list it, then find a qualified buyer, then get the banks to agree, and then risk a deficiency. The odds aren't good.
4. Try to rent the house out to cover the payment which isn't likely without an option to buy and will certainly lead to a bigger mess and enormous grief for the seller. Most are aware and have no intentions of doing so.
5. Enter you, with an ACTS proposal.

What is ACTS?
Back to my example. It's actually very simple. Here's the offer to the seller:
I'll lease-purchase your house for the loan balance at the time it cashes out, and your payment will be made until then. All responsibility for repairs will no longer be yours. I'll need a long-term lease, usually the length of the loan, so your equity has time to return and it can be sold or refinanced. My intent is to find a quality tenant-buyer that you approve before leasing your house,

and I'll collect a fee from them so it costs you nothing.

Many people faced with the choices above will gladly accept this plan and want you to come to their home or go see the house as many are already vacant. Some of them you'll never meet because the paperwork is done by email. More on that in a minute.

Ok, STOP with the skepticism and questions. I told you I'd answer them.

Here goes:
Q: How do I get paid?

A: You collect a simple assignment fee of $5-10k from the buyer and assign them your lease after seller approves.

Q: Can I do this without a license?

A: Yes, as long as you are a principal, and that's why you must first lease-purchase in a company name and then assign. If you have a license this step isn't necessary with full disclosure. You can get paid to find the buyer. You must check with your own attorney on this matter, and I forbid you to do deals until you have. If he/she feels differently you must either not do these deals, get another opinion or get a license.

Q: Why would the buyer pay more than it's worth?

A: Because they get a long-term lease with no pressure to clean up their credit or apply for a bank loan. In fact they may never need a loan. If the buyer leases for say 27 years the debt pay down goes to the buyer. They could literally live in the house until it's paid off and own it at the end. I'm limiting mine to ten years to protect the seller, but that's plenty of time to get the job done and very saleable. They control a beautiful home for long term with a reasonable rent, and the worst that can happen is they live there a few years and move and lose their assignment fee, and most will. *Why Would They Do It, Wouldn't You?* If your answer is no you've never lived in an apartment or with your relatives with screaming kids and little privacy feeling like a low-life. I have, and it's real easy for me to see why your buyer doesn't care about the price. They care about the cash required, the payment and a home of their own. Selling them is easy. The market is huge for buyers. Now add that to the huge sellers' market of over leveraged houses and you can see why everyone's so excited.

Q: Why would the seller allow such a long term?

A: I've actually answered that, but it comes down to them coming to grips with the fact there is no good way out and this is the lesser of all evils. Most people we meet have intentionally decided it's going to foreclosure sooner or later but are still looking for an answer. FYI, most are current on the payments.

Q: Does the seller know what's going on?

A: Absolutely. They get to approve all buyers after we collect a few facts and present them. We approve them first and won't accept obvious future problems and turn down some. Before you create a mental roadblock here you should know the seller will likely approve whomever you approve because no one's making rent payments until they do. FYI, we keep the first rent payment collected at closing of the lease-option as part of our fee in addition to the assignment fee.

Q: What if the tenant tears up the house?

A: Well first, that's less likely with people who put up several thousand to get in, but if they do the seller has instructions to call us and we'll re-lease for them as is. There's a massive amount of buyers who are happy to do the work to get in a home. FYI, all repair responsibility passes on to the tenant buyer in my lease. The seller repairs nothing after the first 30 days.

Q: What if the tenant moves out?

A: They will! The seller simply calls us and we do it again.

Q: What paperwork is involved?

A: Very little. A lease-option agreement, general release from buyer and seller and whatever your attorney wants both sides to sign. That's right, your attorney. Don't you ever think of doing one of these deals without an attorney. Of course I have all the agreements posted on the RonsGoldClub.com membership site, some brand new, all set up for you to email to the seller and your attorney. FYI, the tenant-buyer pays for the attorney.

Q: Does this only work on over leveraged houses?

A: Nope! It works on any terms you create with the seller you can assign to a buyer with seller permission and fully disclosed at original negotiation.

Here's an example:
 ♦ A seller has a free and clear house in great condition worth $200,000 and asking $210,000 but will owner finance with $20,000 down at $1,200 a month.
 ♦ Ok, you know you ain't buying this house, paying too much with a big down payment so normally it's trashed.

But hold on there Buckwheat, you can't make money from trashed deals so here comes the ACTS.

Go ahead and agree to the seller's terms and tell him you'll find a buyer to meet them and assign your contract with his approval. Remember, you must enter into a contract to buy if you don't have a license.

Now you find a buyer who needs owner financing with $25,000 to put down. That means $20,000 goes to the seller and $5,000 goes to you as an assignment fee.

Voilà... a phoenix arises from the ashes and $5,000 appears in your account. I bet your competition don't know this.

Whether it's an over leveraged house, a free and clear house or any other terms you create, you ACTS:

• You never buy the house.
• No money or credit needed.
• No contractors or repairs.
• No banks, loans or private lenders.
• No costly entanglements.

More questions...

Q: What if I don't want to assign the contract but would rather stay in it?

A: Now you're thinking. There are many deals you will want to stay in and sandwich lease. That means you lease with option from the seller and sublease with option to a buyer. This will usually require you to get some free equity and a low payment to seller. If a $200,000 house has a $185,000 debt and a $890 payment and seller will lease-option long term for the loan balance, I may stay in. Now if I get $1,500 rent and a $10,000 non-refundable deposit I just made $11,500 in a few days and $610 a month for years. Why not stay in, especially since all repairs go to the buyer.

Q: What if the house is grossly over leveraged? Like 150%?

A: It depends. If it has a low payment and a potential large monthly spread why not stay in? Let's see, you can make a big assignment fee and collect $500-$1,000 a month possible cash flow for years on a house you don't own. Try that in the stock market and see if you can measure your ROI.

FYI, the more over leveraged, the easier it will be to get the seller to lease to you for the full term of the loan and don't forget, if you stay in, it's you that now owns the house when the loan is paid off with no rent needed. Sleep on that and ask yourself how many of these do you need to retire on the cash flow and really be rich when they pay off.

You see, that house will pay itself off in the same 25-30 years left on the mortgage, even if it's grossly over financed.

Read this again to make sure you clearly understand. It's a game changer, and I know you have more questions so lucky for you all this is in my brand new course called Pretty House Terms and I've now incorporated it into my Quick Start Real Estate School. Plus, I've created a webinar to cover it as well. You'll be notified if you haven't been already.

Tread carefully. This technique must be done right with the correct paperwork and a clear understanding of what questions to ask to get to a conclusion and how to process buyers, which is all included in my system with scripts. I must tell you the live four-day training is by far the best place to get it, and I've built an entire book of scripts.

Tammy Martin, Jacksonville, FL

Dear Ron,

I have been on a "2 year Educational Plan" ever since I first learned about REIA's. Over that period, I have attended 4 bootcamps for various topics and purchased over 10 courses from various other gurus — all were good and I know some were trained by you, if not all!

It is obvious that you are the master, but the thing that really stood out was your live deals in class. This solidified my learning + sort of brought many of the pieces together in a "real-world" setting.

I am so glad I waited and joined your mentoring program instead of someone else's. I already feel 10x closer to the next deals!

Also — Thank you for providing this opportunity to veterans — or else I wouldn't have been here this weekend!

Sincerely,
Tammy Martin

P.S. I have already been telling all my veteran friends in JAX about it!!!

Chapter 3
Eight Myths About Making Money

There are those who always seem to have all the money they could ever need. Then there are those who work and toil all their life and yet never seem to get ahead financially. Which of these two categories do you fall in?

Have you been brainwashed into thinking the only way people get really rich is to inherit a lot of money or just get lucky? The reason most of us think this way is because we haven't been taught by self-made millionaires. Instead, we've learned from those who really don't know a thing about accumulating wealth. The advice you're about to read has been culled from those who have amassed fortunes.

One of the most important points you'll learn is that a surplus of money starts first in the mind. As soon as you understand and can implement this, you will have made a giant step toward true financial prosperity. Here are some myths about money that need to be put to rest now so you can get on with your financial life.

*Myth Number One: *"Financial Security Lies With Having A Good-Paying Job With A Good Company."*

This may not have been a myth 40 years ago, but times have changed. Today, relying on an employer to give you lifelong financial security can be downright dangerous! Unless, of course, you're getting stock options and riding the coattails of a public offering.

What gives you the right to expect your employer will never lay you off someday if the economy takes a downturn? Or what if you're just let go one day because your department has been "reorganized"? Then there's the possibility of your company being bought out by another company, and this new company may decide your position is no longer needed.

True security comes from within, not from someone or something else. We all need to accept personal responsibility for our financial future by building up our own income and cash reserves. Real financial security lies within our own business and not with someone else's business. As long as you're exchanging dollars for hours, your chances of creating true wealth are very slim.

If you ever expect to make real money, you must first put yourself in a position to do so.

*Myth Number Two: *"A Penny Saved Is A Penny Earned."*

This myth doesn't really sound like a myth, does it? In reality, a penny saved is really a penny earned. Saving your spare change will actually add up to a nice little savings after a few years—maybe even enough to buy you a gold watch when you retire. If you want to retire rich, I'd suggest you will take control of your own future and make sure when you check into the nursing home, you own it free and clear.

Do some number crunching and you'll find after you take into account taxes and inflation, any investment that doesn't produce an annual return of at least 10 percent is actually losing money! It pains me to say this, but you can even use your cash to buy real estate and get a much higher return than 10 percent. Of course, if I've trained you, you should know you can get all the real estate you want without using your cash. Then you can put that cash into passive investments to grow at a high rate of return while you actively create cash by buying and selling real estate. Then when you don't want to be active anymore, your passive pot will provide for you the rest of your life.

Money you leave buried in real estate can grow only at the rate that real estate grows, which will be the same whether your cash is buried or freed up to grow passively.

*Myth Number Three: *"All Debt Is Bad."*

Some believe all kinds of debt are bad. However there are two kinds of debt: good debt and bad debt. Consider bad debt as the type that puts you in debt for long periods of time (and in some cases for a lifetime). Run-of-the-mill consumer debt such as charge card debt for jewelry, material trappings, and impulse purchases are examples of bad debt that should be avoided like the plague. For compulsive credit card purchasers whose cards are always at their maximum, the best financial strategy is getting and staying out of bad debt.

So what type of debt is good? Any type of debt for creating wealth is obviously a wise debt. Fortunately, in the real estate business we can buy all the property we want without borrowing money. We simply take over the debt that comes with the property.

There's a big difference between personally guaranteed debt and nonrecourse debt. As you know, I vigorously object to guaranteeing any long-term debt to buy a single-family house. But, I've got folks everywhere making a lot of money by taking over existing debt without recourse ("subject-to"). It's become the mainstream foundation of their business.

This kind of debt produces income. Bad debt produces only outgo. That kind of debt is why we have a country full of job slaves trying to keep up with their bad debt. Let's start thinking like a bank and do more collecting than paying because your debt is producing more revenue than it costs.

*Myth Number Four: *"The Government Will Take Care Of Me."*

Much of our society has been lulled into a false sense of security provided by others. Social Security, unemployment insurance, welfare, food stamps, and other governmental meddling into our lives have created a dependent, "can't-save-myself" class of Americans. This type of pseudo-security has caused great harm to those who have subscribed to it. True security can come only from knowledge, education, confidence, initiative, invention, self-reliance, ability, and innovation. That it comes from others is only an illusion.

Putting too much emphasis on security can be paralyzing. It can cause a person to live in fear, avoid any and all risks, be indecisive, and ultimately live a dull ho-hum life. All things worthwhile in life involve some risk taking: marriage, love, starting your own business, moving to a new city, and so on. Those who don't venture out of their security bubble will never know the true potential of what life can bring.

Some people spend their life playing not to lose instead of playing to win.

*Myth Number Five: *"Failure Is Bad."*

Failure is bad only if you perceive it as such. For those who look at failure as an opportunity to learn and a temporary setback, it can be a building block to bigger and better things. But, many are conditioned to be ashamed of failures and mistakes. This leads to a fear of failure, which becomes a great hindrance to any success that may be looming on the horizon. Those who develop a positive attitude toward failure can conquer the destructive emotions of fear, shame, and guilt. You must be able to put into perspective what others may think about you and continue on your quest for success.

In my experience, the biggest fear is not about failure but the fear of rejection. Most people are worried sick about what others say or think of them. Who cares? It doesn't matter what the morons say. Let them talk, criticize, and complain. The truth is if you knew what was really going on in their life, you wouldn't care what they think. You will fail; I guarantee it. In fact, failure is a prerequisite for success. You see . . .

It's impossible to succeed without failing first.

Life is one failure after another. Those who create wealth simply manage to succeed a few more times than they fail.

*Myth Number Six: *"Being Wealthy Is All About Material Possessions."*

There is more to being wealthy than "he who dies with the most toys wins." There's a huge difference between accumulating money and being wealthy. It's not uncommon for real estate entrepreneurs to become so engulfed with a love for what they're doing they may not realize for months they've become millionaires.

Above all, never pursue money at the expense of your health, peace of mind, loving relationships, and just enjoying personal activities. Money is a means of creating wealth; wealth is a means of creating a great life.

I know this is hard to believe if money's a problem in your life, but real wealth is in the thrill of the chase. Wealth creates power. Power creates more opportunities to be in control. Control creates more chases and therefore more thrills.

You don't need a million bucks in the bank to feel wealthy—you need freedom. Cash flow creates freedom. If you have enough cash coming in you'll begin to feel wealthy, regardless of your bank balance. Now use that cash to generate more, and pretty soon your money's working for you instead of the other way around.

Incidentally, if you've got a million bucks sitting around in a bank account, you've got mush for brains. That's for old ladies and the uneducated who don't understand that banks are paying you less than inflation is costing.

*Myth Number Seven: *"The Acquisition Of Wealth Is A Win/Lose Game."*

If the rich keep getting richer, do the poor keep getting poorer? Thanks to inaccuracies in the media and omissions at our nation's universities, the truth regarding this matter is seldom heard. Here's a bit of reality for you on the situation: You're *not* becoming rich will benefit no one, but your becoming rich benefits others in an abundance of ways.

Wealthy individuals build factories, which create jobs that help the economy. They invest in real estate, which provides housing to renters who cannot afford to buy their own home. They also make tax contributions to the community and support churches, charities, scholarships, and the like. It's a fact the more wealth you create for yourself, the more wealth and opportunities you create for others.

How would you like to live in a country of mostly poor folks? Well, here's some bad news—you do. Folks maybe not at poverty level but barely getting by. Are you one of those folks? If the answer is yes, why? You have no one to blame but yourself. Don't get mad at me; I'm not your boss. I didn't make the conscious decision to be broke; you did. Spend more time creating assets that pay instead of liabilities that suck you dry and your situation will change quickly.

*Myth Number Eight: *"You Must Have Money To Make Money."*

That's the biggest lie since, "the IRS is here to help." People who think this way will die broke. The truth is . . .

If you can't make money without money, you can't make money with money.

Now, I didn't say *no* money was needed. I just said it doesn't have to be your money. You should be using OPM (other people's money), and I wrote this book to show you how to do just that.

The greatest fortunes are made through leverage, and, fortunately, real estate is the highest leveraged vehicle on the planet. Hey, if you don't write a check to buy a house and make money on the deal, your return is infinite. It doesn't get any better than that. That's OPM.

Do you want to be a millionaire? Simply acquire $10 million worth of houses with $9 million of nonrecourse (subject-to) debt and bingo! You're there. Relax, that's only 66 houses worth $150,000 each. What's the big deal? I've got students buying that many houses in one year. What if it took you three or four? Of course, that probably means you're still exchanging hours for dollars. This plan requires you to keep the houses, but what's wrong with that? Buy some, sell some, and keep some. Now you have the best of both worlds.

Wealth is like a house—it needs a good, solid foundation or it will fall apart. People who have taken the time and effort to build solid foundations of successful characteristics can proceed with the business of creating their houses of wealth—doing the framing, laying the bricks, and so forth—with the security that comes from knowing that what they're building is very likely going to last for a long, long time and no one can lay them off or fire them.

Once you know how to buy real estate correctly and understand clearly what to do with it, then you truly have created security. No one can take the knowledge away once you have it.

"You should always buy houses as if you're broke."

Ron LeGrand®

Dale From Flyover Country

I thought I would tell you about a recent deal I did, as I'm in the middle of a divorce I'm not supposed to spend any money or sell anything so don't tell anybody. Back in December the snow was flying and I got bored with nothing to do so I started following some of the on line auctions. I narrowed my search down to some rural areas within commuting distance of a more urban area; these homes seemed to be over looked. It was a two day auction and I watched each of the homes I targeted, nobody bid on one particular home so I waited till about 30 seconds before the close of bidding and placed the next minimum bid, $12500. And Shazam, I was the highest bidder! Although I didn't meet the seller's preset undisclosed minimum acceptable offer, the fine print in the auction rules gives the seller some time to consider and accept your offer. Because I was the highest bidder I still had to put up earnest money so I had to send them $2500/ incase they do accept my bid, two weeks later I was informed that they accepted my offer. Now what? I had to close in thirty days, but I couldn't borrow any money or spend any money cause of the divorce? With the buyer's premium the total price was $15000 and it had to be cash at closing according to the auction rules. Did I mention that this house was 4 hours away! The accessor had it accessed at $130,000, but was realistically worth 60k to 70k as it was a Fannie Mae home I couldn't sell it for a time (seasoning go figure??) So like any good American would do I got a cash advance on a couple of credit cards and set up an ONLINE Closing. Yea I almost never had to leave my home office to close accept I had to go three blocks to have a document notarized. They e-mailed me docs I down loaded signed, rescanned and e-mailed them back. I had already wired the money, so I closed in my own home office. I then put an ad on Craig's list "home for sale contract for deed as is, low down payment" I kinda dragged my feet, but had a buyer lined up in about 30 days. $60,000 with $2,500 down (yea I got my earnest money back) I went on line to one of those legal sites and did a state specific contract for deed for about $12 bucks. I did drive down to meet them to sign at a title company which did not charge me. So with almost no money into it I sold it for $60,000 less the down payment equal to my earnest money, I financed $57,500 for 15 years @6.5% interest with a payment of $500.89. So bottom line is $60000 less purchase of $15000 equals $45000 profit plus don't forget the interest of $32,659.61 over 15 years. That's a total profit of $77,659.61 without hardly leaving my house. (Ok I did go there twice once to hang a lock box and once to close) Cash flow can be just as important as a lump sum' this will almost pay for my daughters collage in one deal. Shhhh don't tell my soon to be X

Dale from Flyover county...............................

Chapter 4
Everyone Wins Or I Won't Play

Some outsiders are under the impression the only way to make money in quick turn real estate is to take advantage of people. They picture all of us investors' literally stealing houses and putting old ladies out on the street, or they perceive us as tyrannical landlords wearing big black hats operating slum properties unfit for human habitation. Such perceptions are not just erroneous—they demonstrate total ignorance.

In all the years I've been an investor buying more than 3,000 houses, not once have I ever put a gun to a seller's head and said, "Sign or die." In fact, many times I've found myself hoping the seller wouldn't work with me because I didn't like the looks of a deal, but I went ahead and bought anyway to get the seller out of a jam. That's not what I'd suggest you do. It's better to walk.

Many people don't understand the valuable services real estate entrepreneurs perform for the public. Of course, I wouldn't buy a house if I couldn't make a profit from it, but in many cases I could have walked away and been happier than if I had bought. However, the seller's needs pushed me to take on some project or other that many not have been the best use of my time.

In looking at the real estate business, several elements must be considered. First, the business is more than money. Money is only the by-product of a specialized activity that provides one of life's necessities—shelter. Think about the last sad story you heard about a family home lost to foreclosure. Maybe you, yourself, have been through hard times and lost your house to a bank. How would you have felt about an investor's providing you with a solution when no one else could or would? I can tell you from experience few things in life are more humiliating and stressful than having lenders hounding you almost daily, demanding payments you can't cough up.

Going through that process destroys self-esteem, breaks up marriages, and can even cause health problems—or worse. I once bought a house whose owner—the father of three children—had committed suicide under the stress of pending foreclosure. That experience gave me a new outlook on life. At the same time, I was buying the widow's house at eight o'clock one Saturday night, and trying to help her stop crying, when I decided my measly little problems didn't amount to a hill of beans compared with hers.

She had three kids, but she had no income, no job, no food, and now no husband. All of a sudden I switched from the mind-set of "How cheaply can I get this house?" to "How much can I afford to give this lady?" She owed $26,000 on a $50,000 house (remember this was in the early 1980s), and the monthly payment was $280. She was four months behind on her payments, and the house needed about $2,000 in repairs. She told me if I would give her $1,000 and make up her payments, she would deed the house to me.

Now I'm no angel, and I'm usually pretty reluctant to give up a buck unless it's absolutely necessary, but that night was an exception. I reached into my wallet and handed her $500 cash. Then, I told her once I had checked her title and she was out of the house, I would give her an additional $3,500. That's $3,000 more than she was asking. Needless to say, she was elated, and I had won a friend for life.

But, who really got the best bargain? Yes, I made money on the house and could have made $3,000 more. But the most important result of the deal: I was on a high for weeks afterward, and I had learned a lesson that will stick with me for life—*You can't help someone up a hill without getting closer to the top yourself!*

Remembering that experience still gives me goose bumps. And, I'm sure as your career progresses, you'll have the opportunity to help a similar family solve its problems.

➤ Saving Houses From The Wrecking Ball

In addition to the human element, of course, there's also the matter of the houses themselves. Think of all the houses that are rehabbed by investors every week. If investors don't buy them, who will? What happens to them?

The answer is they get bulldozed, or they just sit there until they are boarded up and condemned, then fall down on their own. True, every once in a while an owner-occupant buys a property to fix up and occupy. But for every one of those, 100 got rehabbed for profit by people like us. We're providing a service to our community by improving the looks of the neighborhood, as well as by increasing the stock of the houses and the community's tax base. That, in turn, generates more revenue for the city.

In addition, rehabbing requires contractors and laborers who benefit from the work. All rehabs require more materials, which are supplied by vendors who buy from manufacturers—all businesses that create jobs and employ people. And, the process generates fees for professionals such as surveyors, Realtors®, appraisers, termite inspectors, closing agents, title clerks, attorneys, and so on. Stop the rehabbing of houses, and all those people would suffer directly or indirectly; many couldn't exist. So yes, people who buy and fix houses are certainly performing a public service.

➢ Sharing The Wealth

Let's look at aspects of real estate investing that have nothing to do with the rehabbing process itself. Have you ever known people who have had to make two house payments simultaneously because they purchased a new home before the old one was sold?

Who besides an investor is going to offer debt relief when the house doesn't sell? Real estate brokers? Hardly. Realtors® attempt to sell houses at little or no risk to themselves. Making a seller's payments while tying up a house for six months is not part of their service.

Could a seller rent the house to a tenant? Possibly. More often than not, all the seller would wind up with is an expensive lesson in landlording and a bigger problem. Renting the house could also make it extremely difficult to sell. It would rarely be clean, and getting access to it would be complicated. Of course, the tenant would not be cooperating with the seller if it meant that when the house was sold the tenant would have to move.

So, we investors step in and take over payments and repairs, and we usually get the house sold in time. The seller's problem is solved, and we have provided a valuable service.

Believe it or not, while we're working to help sellers by saving them from the foreclosure machinery of the big bad banks, we're also performing a service for those banks. And, that service, too, trickles down to a wider public. If investors didn't buy houses out of foreclosure or afterward, who would? If the only market were owner-occupants, you would see a drastic decline in housing prices. Moreover, the conditions for getting a loan would become terribly stringent. Those factors would slow demand drastically, and all related industries would suffer, many of them evaporating.

Yet another very important group of people benefit from investors' work in real estate. What about all those owner-occupants who wouldn't have a home of their own without us? I have sold hundreds of houses to first-time, and last-time homebuyers. Many of them needed help solving minor problems and overcoming hurdles. I can honestly say some would never have been able to buy had I not made it possible.

Sometimes I helped them get financing. Sometimes I was the bank and owner financed for them. Without my being the bank and allowing them to bypass rigorous qualifying procedures, most of these people would still be renters today. Usually, investors are the only owner—financing game in town.

Without us, owner-financing would be almost nonexistent.

So are we providing a public service by understanding creative financing? You bet. We are providing a service that is extremely important to those families who couldn't own a home any other way. Incidentally, if it weren't for investors who would own rental property, and where would all the tenants live?

True, as you become more and more involved with real

estate investing, you may get the feeling you're not always appreciated. Sometimes we get a lot of flak from government employees, real estate professionals, and other people who don't understand the business. But, rest assured investors will be around as long as people need places to live. There is plenty of business to go around, and investors can make money without making anyone suffer. If any deal is not win-win, just don't do it. Move on.

"You can't help someone get up a hill without getting closer to the top yourself."

H. Norman Schwarzkopf

Dorien and Rineke Forster-New Zealand

Dear Ron,

You truly are now world famous! This is a big thank you from your fans half way around the world in New Zealand. When we met you we were just typical small time "buy and hold" investors. We have been flying around the world many times to hang around you and your people to learn new ideas to bring to our country. That was a good idea!

After changing some of the contracts to our local laws, we have done some great deals and also now have run three successful seminars. Needless to say, thanks to you and your wonderful courses we are now "full time unemployed Property entrepreneurs." Our live style has changes dramatically after meeting you and there is no going back!!

As a result of teaching our property portfolio has increased three fold. We have several lease options and have been able to help others with new concepts. The cost and travel involved for attending your courses from New Zealand has been well worth it!!

A bit thank you from us and other "sheeple" in New Zealand. We look forward and wish you well to your new courses and ideas. Let us know what and when and we will be in the front row again. You are the best!

Your Kiwi girls from New Zealand,

Dorien and Rineke Forster

Part Two

It's time to get paid

Chapter 5
Five ways to profit

Quick turn transactions fall into five main categories: (1) rehabbing and retailing; (2) wholesaling; (3) getting the deed; (4) lease-options; and (5) options. Almost everything you do in the real estate investing business will follow one of these methods.

➢ *Rehabbing And Retailing*

Buying houses low and selling them high is called *retailing*. This is the most easily understood method of investing in real estate because of the countless books and tapes on the subject. It's the art of buying at a low price, often doing some repairs, and then selling at retail price and usually cashing out. A lot of money is made through this method. Some people do it part-time, turning two or three houses a year, and make more money at it than they make on their regular jobs. Others do it full-time and turn 40 to 80 houses a year with an average profit from $20,000 to $35,000 per deal.

In the following chapters you'll find a plan for locating these basically ugly houses, making offers, estimating repairs and selling quickly. If you attempt to do this type of deal from a book, I have to caution you a lot can go wrong, but obviously I can't cover every detail here. Rehabbing and retailing houses is very profitable, but it's also the hardest way to make money in real estate and is layered with costly entanglements. Frankly, it's not where I'd suggest you start your career unless you simply can't control that internal burning desire to make something ugly into something pretty.

A lot of satisfaction comes from rehabbing, and there's a lot to learn. However, if you have a choice to make money an easy way or a hard way, my guess is you'd take the easy way; I know I would. In fact, the older I get, the easier I want it.

But if you can't resist the urge to buy and renovate, here are some tips not covered in later chapters:

Tip 1. Buy in areas where qualified buyers want to live, not in war zones where bullets fly and little white bags change hands on street corners.

Tip 2. Pay close attention to my MAO (maximum allowable offer) formula in Chapter 7 and buy well below the MAO. If you pay too much for the house, you'll be working for nothing—or worse.

Tip 3. Never close your purchase without confirming your assumptions, which are after repaired value, and repair estimates. Do your due diligence and get the purchase appraised as completed, buy title insurance, have a termite inspection, get repair estimate(s) from qualified contractors, and get estimates to fix any other traps you can avoid.

Tip 4. Always borrow more than you need to buy and repair. The job will always cost more, take longer, and yield less profit than you expect. You better have a cash reserve. Chapter 11 covers where to get the money to buy "junkers" even if you're dead broke, bankrupt, and have bad breath, BO, and no friends or family and just got released from the federal penitentiary.

Tip 5. Keep a tight leash on contractors. They'll play you like a yo-yo, which can—and probably will—be one of your biggest learning experiences in The School of Hard Knocks. But, hey, don't worry. I graduated from that same school top of my class, and I survived.

Tip 6. Don't tie up your cash. Tying it up is a good way to become a motivated seller. The greater your need to sell, the longer it will take. Ron's law!

Tip 7. Do a nice renovation job. It'll pay handsome dividends in saved holding costs and in satisfied customers who'll send you more buyers.

Tip 8. Find a good loan processor or mortgage broker to get your buyers financed. It's the difference between success and failure. This person has your paycheck in his or her control, so make sure the person you find knows his or her business and follows up.

Tip 9. Master the art of selling houses as fast as humanly possible. Slow selling is the biggest weakness for most yet one of the easiest to fix. If you sell houses the way most untrained investors do. It'll be a while before you get paid.

Tip 10. Never do your own repairs. If you do, you're working as a laborer, not an investor. You make money by locating and buying good deals, not swinging a paint brush. If you adhere to Tip 4, it won't be a problem; you'll have the money. Some people tell me fixing houses is their therapy. I say if you lay your hands on a house, you need therapy.

Tip 11. Get trained at this craft of quick turning real estate before you have to pay an ugly price for your education. Education is a lot cheaper than ignorance.

Go to **www.RonQuickStart.com** and check out our four-day.

➢ *Wholesaling*

The second method of investing in real estate is wholesaling. This is an entire business in itself and generates super-fast profits, usually without ever acquiring the title on the property. It's not uncommon to pick up a check at closing with the seller and buyer present at the same time. Many times I have earned thousands of dollars within two or three days of finding a deal. Successful people in the wholesale business are accomplished at locating good deals and marketing them—primarily to people who are in the rehabbing and retailing business. The first purchaser is willing to take a smaller, fast profit and leave the larger profit to an investor with the time and money to buy, repair, and sit on the house until it's sold.

Some of my students are making a good income by buying and then reselling immediately only once or twice a month. These deals require no money, no credit, and no bosses. Believe me, if you locate a deal someone is waiting to buy it from you. Finding bargains for bargain hunters is the easiest and quickest way I know to pick up a check for at least $5,000. The whole process shouldn't take more than 15 to 20 days from the beginning to the end.

In Chapter 6 I discuss ways to find these junkers, and Chapter 10 covers selling them quickly. The only difference between wholesaling and retailing is in the exit strategy you use. It's the same house—ugly!

Here are some wholesaling tips not discussed in detail in later chapters:

Tip 1. Don't pay too much. Remember, you're selling to bargain hunters. Leave them plenty of room to make a profit or you won't find a buyer. That means they should net at least 20 percent of the sales price after all expense.

Tip 2. If the house is in a war zone, you better be paying war zone prices. "Buy 'em so cheap you can sell 'em so cheap your buyers can't refuse 'em." The biggest market is landlords looking for low-income rentals. Buy well below the MAO discussed in Chapter 7.

Tip 3. Your only exit is to sell for all cash quickly. Make sure your buyers can get the cash and aren't relying on bank financing. Don't allow buyers to learn banks won't finance junkers at your expense. If a buyer can't close in 15 days or less, find another buyer.

Tip 4. Use an assignment of contract and let your closing agent collect your fee. See Chapter 10 for details and Appendix A for the assignment.

There's really not that much to learn about wholesaling. It's an easy business. I have students all over North America doing one-to-ten deals a month and netting a low of $3,000.

Some make more on one wholesale deal than most people make in a year on their job.

➢ Getting The Deed

The third method of real estate investing involves acquiring ownership of houses by taking over the existing debt. The common term used is a "*subject-to clause*"—you take title subject-to the underlying financing. This method doesn't involve credit because you are not assuming the loan. Title stays in the seller's name but transfers to you. This is the most common technique used by real estate investors today and is literally making millionaires all over the free world.

The normal exit strategy is to sell for cash to a qualified buyer immediately or to install a lease-purchase tenant until that tenant gets financed at a later date, a topic I cover in Chapter 10.

To use the "subject-to" clause requires you to go beyond what you may consider normal or reasonable. There are three issues some people have a hard time coping with here, and they keep a lot of folks from reaching the big profits. Get past them and it's worth a fortune to you. These are the three issues:

1. ***People deed their house to you and the loan stays in their name.*** You'll get the house, but you will not assume the debt or accept the personal responsibility. Instead, you'll **take over the debt**, which is called taking title **"subject-to."** The loan shows on the seller's credit report until it's paid off, and yes, the seller's credit is in your hands. The only kind of seller who will do this is one that *needs* to sell, *not wants* to sell (more on this in Chapter 6). The need to sell must outweigh the concern about credit or you won't get the deed. Some sellers couldn't care less about their credit—it's already shot before they call you. Other sellers have good credit but want debt relief now and simply believe you'll do what you say. There is no written personal guarantee on your part, and you are only morally obligated to do what you promise you'll do.

2. ***People give you thousands of dollars in free equity if you let them.*** Equity is "pie-in-the-sky" money that doesn't exist until the property is cashed out at retail price. Debt relief and

a long list of other motivating factors compel many people to give away equity in exchange for peace of mind. If you understand this and stop trying to psychoanalyze other people's motives, you can quickly amass millions in free equity that you can turn into cash with a little training.

3. The lender can call the loan due because the title transferred without the loans being paid off. There's a due-on-sale clause in all loans now that gives lenders this right. That's the bad news. The good news is that lenders hate real estate—it's a plague to them. They're in the money business. Rarely will lenders call a loan due when someone is willing to make the payments, and that's assuming they even learn it transferred before they get paid off.

But, let's play worst-case scenario. If the lender did call it due, that won't affect your credit. You didn't guarantee the note. No one will be knocking on your door collecting your assets, except for this house. Your name wouldn't be mentioned in a lawsuit unless you are foolish enough to take title in your own name. (More on this in Chapter 13 on land trusts.)

Will the lender's calling the loan due affect the seller's credit? Yes, it will. That's why I or my students never get a deed "subject-to" without also getting what I call a CYA letter signed by the seller. It's a simple disclosure whereby the seller acknowledges having been made aware the loan will stay in the seller's name and that the bank could call the loan due. Any sellers who'll deed you their house will sign a CYA letter; if not, don't take the house.

We'll cover how to buy and sell these extremely profitable and easy-to-do deals in later chapters. Try to overcome your objections and apprehensions here and keep an open mind. I have over 500,000 students to date, and I'd bet over 60 percent of them have bought free houses on a subject-to basis. Who knows, it might even work for you. I've bought over 400 houses "subject-to" and not once has a lender called the loan due.

➤ Lease-Options (Includes ACTS From Chapter 2)

The fourth method of investing in real estate is to *lease-option* properties from sellers to control the properties without taking title. This method works on houses in any price range and with any underlying financing. You can reap big profits without ever owning the house while at the same time paying no closing costs to buy or sell, doing no repairs, and using very little or no money.

The objective is to either sell for cash or install a tenant-buyer to lease-purchase from you until he or she cashes out or until you can cash out immediately by getting enough free equity. This technique is sometimes referred to as a *"sandwich lease."* You're the meat in the sandwich.

Buying with a lease-option overcomes all the objections I just discussed because the title doesn't go from the seller to you until your buyer gets new financing in the future. Therefore, a bank can't call the loan due and the seller's credit is not in your hands. However, you must still get free equity, or there's no reason to get involved.

You'll find and sell these deals the same way you do all the others. The only difference is you're leasing instead of buying. Your agreement must give you the right to buy at a fixed price—usually the loan balance—and the right to sublet to a tenant. You totally control the property during this term you agree to, and the seller can't reverse the agreement unless you default. It's truly control without ownership.

You should only lease-option attractive houses ready to be occupied, and the maximum deposit to the seller is $100. If the seller wants more money, get the deed or get the door.

Honestly, in today's market it's easy to get the deed, and I'd rather have ownership than control for two main reasons:

1. When I get a deed, I never have to contact the seller again for any permission or signature. I own the house just as legally, morally and ethically as if I had paid cash, but that's not true for lease-options. The seller in a lease-option transact can always be a problem later after you've solved the problem and are about ready to cash out.

2. I can depreciate a house I own, but I can't depreciate one I lease. On a house I bought for $150,000 (the loan amount I took over), that came to about $5,000 a year
I get for free through a tax write-off.

When people call you to buy their house, they usually want to sell, not rent it. Buying is a conclusion, even if the loan is in their name. Of course, there are times when lease-optioning makes sense—perhaps it's the only way you'll get the deal, so you should be prepared. All it takes is a little training and a couple of agreements to be in business—a multi-million-dollar business I might add.

➤ Options

Using the *options* method of investing, you simply agree to option a property at a price A with the intent to sell at Price B. You hope that price B is higher than price A; the difference is your profit. This is a risk-free technique that's producing huge paychecks for some of my students. The biggest as of this writing is from an Orlando, Florida student who made $2,450,000 *on one deal in 43 days with a $100 investment.*

His name is Marco Kozlowski, a 30-something guy I stole from the job market and turned into an assassin. In his first year in business, Marco acquired 119 deeds on "pretty" houses in the Orlando area. Then, he started raising his sights and working with ultra-expensive houses. Once he learned it doesn't cost a nickel more or take any more time or resources or risk to deal with multi-million-dollar houses as it does to deal with hundred-thousand-dollar houses, there was no stopping Marco.

He found a wealthy guy who had an $8,600,000 house on the market for four years with a Realtor®. It was vacant, and one of five the guy owned; at that price it was obviously a pretty cool pad with all the bells and whistles, including a dock and waterfront. After three months of going back and forth, the seller agreed to option the house to Marco for $4,000,000. So much for our previous discussion about getting free equity! This house was a pain to the seller; he didn't want or need it, and the money meant nothing to him. In addition, he had a $5,000,000 yacht parked at the dock. Marco optioned the house for $4,000,000 and got a bunch of free "stuff" in the house with the deal. His total deposit was $100 to the seller. He later admitted he forgot to even give him that.

Marco then called an auctioneer to call some end consignment houses in order to load the place up with art, furniture, and other stuff to sell at the auction with the house and the yacht.

Over 300 people attended the two-day auction. The house sold for $5,600,000, the yacht for $4,300,000, and the stuff for almost $1,000,000. Marco netted $2,400,000 altogether on this one deal, with no money, no credit, no risk, and no promises he couldn't keep. I was with him the day he got the wire transfer from the closing. He was a mental wreck all day until it came.

Actually, options are nothing more than retailing a house for cash. You simply bypass the repair process and remove all risks. When you think about retailing houses to an owner-occupant, you usually conjure up all the negative things that come with that part of our business. Where do I get the money to buy and fix the house? What if I underestimate the repair costs? Where do I find a good contractor who'll work cheap? What if my contractor stiffs me? What if I can't sell the house? How do I make payment on a vacant house if I'm barely surviving now?

I bet you could throw a few more fears in the pot. In fact, within the next few pages you'll learn what could be a full-time (or part-time) business that could easily—and I really mean *easily* -net you more money than your job does.

Not only will you make more money, but we'll eliminate the following negatives while we're at it:

- I need money. (*You won't need much.*)
- I need credit. (*You won't borrow a cent.*)
- Repairs scare me. (*You won't be doing any.*)
- I'm afraid the house won't sell. (*If it doesn't, you won't*

lose a nickel.)

- ◆ I don't want anyone mad at me. (*No one will be because you won't make anyone any promises or commitments.*)
- ◆ I can't make payments. (*You won't have any to make.*)
- ◆ I'm afraid I'll lose. (*Lose what? If you have nothing invested and no promises to break, how can you lose?*)
- ◆ But I don't know how to sell houses. (*Maybe this would be a good place to learn, as there is no way to lose.*)
- ◆ I just don't know; even though I can't lose, I'm scared. (*It's better to be scared and moving than afraid and frozen.*)

Let's talk about why you would want to retail houses in the first place. Actually, there's only one good reason I can think of from my 30 years in the business and retailing about 700 houses. When I say *retail*, I mean all cash to qualified buyers who paid full price and need new financing. I'm not counting all the owner financing deals in this number or the 500-plus wholesale deals.

The reason I elected to go the retail route on these 700 houses was because the payoff was large enough to make it worth the effort it takes to find a qualified buyer and get that buyer to the closing table.   Even in the beginning, that represented a minimum of $10,000 per house. Now, I just won't retail a house unless it has a minimum of $30,000 net—not gross—profit.

If I lived in a higher-priced market where the cheapest "bread-and-butter" houses started at $200,000, for example, I wouldn't settle for $30,000. I want a minimum of 20 percent of the sales price as a profit, and the truth is that I usually get closer to 30 to 40 percent. In fact, that net profit figure is the biggest factor in determining whether to wholesale or to retail the house.

Now, don't go off the deep end on me when I start talking about a 30 to 40 percent profit. If you're new, you won't believe it. If you've been around a while and aren't doing the same, you need some fine-tuning. I went back and figured out my last six houses for this book. I was rather shocked myself to find out my average net profit on those six deals was a whopping

33 percent. That's one-third of the sales price in my pocket. I actually bought, repaired, and maintained all six of these houses until they were sold. In the technique I discuss here, you won't buy or maintain or repair. Therefore, I think it's reasonable for you to be willing to work for less than 33 percent because you'll have no money invested and no risk at all.

Once you learn the system involved in the business of retailing, I think you'll agree with me that it's a business well worth your time to learn. Once you learn how to do it with options instead of ownership, I think you'll agree it just doesn't get better than this. No risk, no money, no credit, and no way to lose. Of course, some people prefer to actually buy and fix because they just like to make pretty something that's ugly. I can understand that; somebody's got to fix those junkers.

But, now let's explore an alternative plan. How many houses can you find that fit the following descriptions?

- ◆ Vacant or soon to be
- ◆ Great neighborhood in any price range (in fact, the higher the better)
- ◆ Owner will sell for 20 percent or more below market for all cash
- ◆ A house in excellent condition and ready to occupy

You think maybe there might be a few of these sitting around? The answer is absolutely! More than you'll ever be able to handle, so point number one is *spend your time on prime prospects only*. A prime prospect is a well-located house in a fast-moving area that's in excellent condition. No projects wanted here. No hurdles to overcome, like smelly carpet, poor landscaping, or other deferred maintenance. No war zones where qualified people don't want to live and no trashy neighborhoods.

OK, Ron, I'm waiting to learn what I'm supposed to do with these gorgeous houses and how I make money if I'm not going to buy them. *The answer in a word is options.* You see, you don't need to own a house to profit from it. Suppose you own a home worth $200,000 and owe $148,000 to a bank. You work for a large corporation and just got transferred out of state effective in 60 days. Your house payment is $1,285 per month and you're doing OK as long as that's your only payment. But when you move, making a payment on both houses will be a crippling blow. You're thinking about listing with a Realtor® and see my ad in the paper:

I'll Buy Your Home & Pay You Cash, Any Price Range, 555-1212

You call my ad and quickly learn the only way I can help you is to offer you my lease-option program, giving you two choices. The first choice is that I'll lease-option your home, make your payments, and eventually sell the home for cash. I'll need an agreed-on strike price equaling your loan balance when I sell and the right to sublease to a tenant-buyer.

You quickly make me aware that your house is too pretty to allow me to rent it out. You just won't sleep at night knowing a tenant lives in your beautiful home. OK, I say. I understand that. So here's plan two: I'll simply option your house for $148,000 all cash. No terms! No long-term option and no right to sublease.

All I want from you is a key so I can show it and the right for me or my assigns to buy it. I need only a six-month option. I'll advertise your house at my own expense. I'll think about it every day when I get up and when I go to bed and personally work on it until it's sold or the six months expire.

Heck, since you're leaving town I'll even keep your lawn mowed at my expense for the whole time. The downside is that because you won't let me sublease the house I can't make any of your monthly payments while I'm selling your house.

OK, that's your offer. Now let's go through all the objections a seller could come up with to our plan two proposal:

Q. *Why should I let you tie up my house?*

A. Good question, but what if I don't tie up your house? Let's do this: I'll put it in the agreement that if you sell your house before I do, I'll cancel the agreement and go on my merry way. You'll owe me nothing. Is that fair?

Q. *Does this mean you will try to sell my house for me, but I'm still free to sell it myself?*

A. Yes, that's exactly what I mean.

Q. *Don't you need a license to do this?*

A. No! Not as long as you have a written option agreement. When the seller signs the agreement, you have been given an equitable interest in the house that gives you every right to sell, especially because your seller has granted that right as well. When you have an equitable interest in a property, in most states you don't need a license to sell it. You should verify this with your attorney.

Q. *How large a deposit will you give me?*

A. Well, Mr. Seller, let me ask you this: When you list with your Realtor®, how large a deposit does the Realtor® give you? None, of course. Then why should I? All I'm asking is the right to buy and a key to show the house. As I'm not even taking the house off the market or occupying it, how can you lose? Why do you need a deposit?

Q. *How long an option do you want?*

A. Well, let's see. How long do you want to give me, considering I'll go away anytime you sell, and you have no risk and nothing to lose? Frankly, all I need is six months. If I haven't sold it by then, I'm "gonna" move on anyway.

This is by no means a full-fledged course on options, but it certainly gets you thinking, doesn't it? Let's see what we've accomplished with our make-believe deal. We've taken control of a $200,000 house in good condition with no money, no credit, no promises to keep, and no risk. If we sell the house, we make about $50,000. If we don't, we lose nothing except the cost of an ad. We didn't deal with any contractors or rehabbers. No monthly payments to worry about and no tenants.

What's more, the seller decided which plan we used. Plan one, whereby we leased with the right to sublease, or plan two, whereby we don't have the right to occupy but do get paid if we sell it.

Looks to me like this just might be the perfect business. The only downside is that you must know how to retail houses for cash. When you put together a system for doing so, I think you'll agree with me, based on this discussion, that optioning houses is by far the best way to acquire maximum short-term cash profits.

Incidentally, don't get hung up on my $200,000 example. You can work with any price range you like—no minimum and no maximum. But remember, it doesn't take any longer to get a buyer through the system whether you net $200,000 or $100,000 or, like my hero, Marco, $2,450,000.

Be careful not to spend your time walking over the dollars to get to the dimes. If I were you, I'd work on the highest-priced houses in your area that are moving quickly. It's common sense: The higher the values, the better chance you have of negotiating a larger profit. That's contrary to those junkers, isn't it? When you actually have to buy the house and pay holding, repair, and sales costs. I'd be concerned if you dealt with anything other than the cheap houses.

When you have nothing at risk, you can play for higher stakes.

All right, I know I said in the beginning you didn't need a cent to do this, and then I talked about advertising. OK, you need a few bucks. But, wouldn't you feel more comfortable if advertising money was all you had to risk? Or would you prefer having to buy a house, come up with the repair money, hire contractors, pay property taxes, insurance, and utilities, and then get stuck if the house didn't sell quickly? Sounds like a no-brainer to me. Options are a lot safer than owning.

Besides, if you'll allow your mind to go beyond my $200,000 example for a minute, you'll realize this will work on million-dollar houses as well. Wherever you live, there are executive homes worth several hundred thousand dollars more than the seller would accept for a cash sell. Yes, this means you can make $100,000 per house or more. It's your choice. If the numbers scare you, ask yourself . . .

"What have I got to lose?"

I promise when you get a check in your hands for $100,000, you'll discover options are not only worth your time to learn but they pay better than any job where you swap hours for dollars. If you agree and want to learn more, I have a training event called **Pretty House Terms** where I cover many little-known techniques, including options, lease-options, structuring offers, answering objections, agreements, and a lot more. Call my office for more information at **800-567-6128** or go to **www.RonsQuickStart.com.**

➢ *Pretty Houses And Ugly Houses*

The real estate investing business is actually divided into only two parts: pretty houses and ugly houses. Retailing and wholesaling involve finding houses that need to be rehabbed. They're ugly. Some need more than $20,000 in work and others need less, but all need repairs. That's why you can buy them at deeply discounted prices.

Lease-options, options, and get-the-deed houses are pretty houses needing little or no work. They're in gorgeous areas and in all price ranges from $75,000 to $5 million.

The focus for ugly houses is to buy them cheap. Price is king. Usually it's an all-cash offer. The focus for pretty houses is to take over debt and get some free equity or option and resell. Because little or no cash is required to buy, you usually get less equity than you do in an all-cash offer on junkers, but it's easy in and out because you don't have to raise cash or hire contractors

Both types of houses have advantages and disadvantages, you may have already formed an opinion about what you'd like to do to create big checks in real estate, but don't be too hasty. All of these techniques work and all should be in your toolbox. We'll discuss each in this book.

Some people ask me what they should look for first,

pretty houses or ugly houses. My answer is always this: "Find a seller who needs to sell and help that seller whether the house is pretty or ugly." When you get a check from the closing agent, it won't have a note on it anywhere saying this money came from a pretty or ugly house.

I'd like you to learn the whole business, not just a little piece of it as some do. When you can take whatever comes to you—pretty or ugly—and profit from it, you have become what I call a "transaction engineer" and have joined the elite in our business who truly understand it. You can't find pretty houses without finding ugly ones too, and vice versa. Don't go through a whole career as a real estate entrepreneur with blinders on and throw away a dollar for every dime you harvest. Spend a little time and money to learn your craft correctly, and you'll need only a few prospects a month to make a fortune.

The only other alternative is to learn and work one type of deal and spend all your time looking for a needle in a haystack. Remember, **_The Less I Do, the More I Make._** That starts with recognizing opportunity when it's thrown at you and being savvy enough to grab it.

"Leverage your brain, not your

wallet or credit."

Ron LeGrand®

Dan Knowles- Flemington, NJ

Dear Ron,

I attended your Quick Start Real Estate School in New Jersey. I was a broke real estate agent at the time. With your help and ideas, I was able to close my first investor deal, and I walked away with $30,000. I almost passed out at the closing table when the title clerk handed me my check.

I also received a $3,700 real estate check paid to my broker. Not a bad deal, $33,700 on one house. I cannot thank you enough, Ron! You changed my life, and I thank you every $100 bill I count!

Thanks!

Dan Knowles

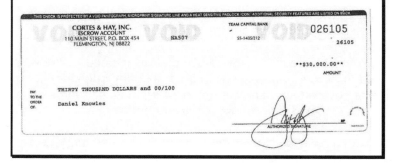

Chapter 6
Five Steps To Success

This business and all others have five steps that must be followed to succeed. If any one is eliminated, the business will suffer or fail outright. If you currently run a business or have in the past and it had problems, I'd suggest you take a good hard look at my five steps, and I'll bet you'll spot the problem.

I spend a major portion of the book covering these steps and incorporate a mini-real estate training school in the art of buying and selling houses. The information in the next chapters took a lot of years to learn and is the foundation for all my millionaires and will remain so for future generations.

➢ *Caution, Caution, Caution*

No book on any shelf can give you a complete education on anything. This one is no exception. The purpose of this book is to awaken the financial genius inside you and make you aware of the fabulous opportunity out there in real estate.

To assume this book is all you'll ever need to know is naive and borders on insanity. I could take any one chapter on subjects covered here and create an entire book or course on it. In fact, I've done that for most of the content.

You have available to you complete home study courses called "Cash Flow Systems," which contain thirty-seven CDs and systems manuals on both the pretty and the wholesale and retail business. In addition, we have a four-day live training on both parts of the business. They're taught about six times a year all over the country and Canada. Then we have personal mentoring by phone and in person on a one-on-one basis.

In fact, we have a whole curriculum of live training events to cover every need in real estate and marketing so our clients can move up as far and as fast as they choose. It's all on **www.RonLeGrand.com** for you to check out and is called Financial Freedom Academy.

Yes, that was a shameless commercial, but I hope it

clearly illustrates that no book can ever make you an expert on anything. I'd prefer you didn't take the information in this book and implement it with no further training. I know that's not what you may want to hear but it's the truth.

This business can make you wealthy very quickly, so please give it the time and attention it deserves if you enter it, and do yourself a favor and don't expect miracles from a book. I'm sure glad the doctor who did surgery on me recently didn't get all his training from a book.

OK, my disclaimer is over, so let's get back to the five steps of success. Each is covered in the next five chapters and is applied to both the pretty and the ugly houses as we go. I said earlier that the pretty and wholesale and retail business are actually two different businesses within one. There are a few similarities but, by and large, they're quite different. Even so, the steps to success are the same. Here they are:

Step 1.   **Locate prospects**

Step 2.   **Prescreen prospects**

Step 3.   **Construct and present offers**

Step 4.   **Follow up**

Step 5.   **Sell quickly**

Now let's see how to apply these steps to buying and selling a house with no money or credit and getting a big fat check quickly.

"Focus on the few, not the many. It matters not how many deals you do, only how much money you make."

Ron LeGrand®

Christian Whittier, Salt Lake City, Utah

Dear Ron,

My name is Christian Whittier and I attended your seminar in Salt Lake City, Utah. Wow!!! What an eye opener. When I received your course, I spent the next 3 days listening to it but I got so motivated I had to get out there and make some offers before I could even finish listening to it. I made 6 offers before one was accepted. I made some goals to reach for 30 days after your seminar, and with your help I accomplished all of them!

Thanks for all of the help and motivation. I'm looking forward to your boot camps.

Sincerely,
Christian Whittier

Chapter 7
Step 1 - Locating Prospects

Every business must locate people to buy its products and services or it'll soon be out of business. In our case we must locate people who have houses for sale so we can buy their product, a house.

That's not a hard process, but it's deadly if it doesn't get done. In fact, when I converse with students who aren't doing well, it usually comes down to one of two reasons: Either they haven't done much to find deals or they're finding them and letting them get by because they don't recognize what a deal looks like. I'll fix that in the next chapter.

Before I go any further we should discuss the use of Realtors®. It's easy to pin all your hopes on them and assume they'll do most of the work for you. Sorry! Bad news! The only time you'll use Realtors® is to make offers on listed junkers. Realtors® won't be used in the pretty house business for two reasons.

First, they want to get paid, and most pretty house deals are debt takeovers or options. There's no money to pay Realtors®. The seller gets little or nothing, so the deals are cashless.

The second reason Realtors® won't be used in the pretty house business is the biggest roadblock: Realtors® won't advise their clients to sell the way you want to buy. They'll block the sale and destroy the deal if it involves taking over debt without liability (get the deed) or involves options, usually lease-options— all buying techniques in the pretty home business.

Your only market therefore for pretty houses to buy is through FSBOs (for sale by owners). Here you must deal with the seller directly, and all listed properties are off-limits unless the seller can convince the Realtor® to drop the listing. Note that I said the seller, not you, must contact the Realtor®; if you do, the Realtor® will most likely want to be paid if you buy the house. Realtors® have a contract (listing agreement), and you mustn't interfere with it unless the Realtor® chooses to cancel it to help the seller. Violate this rule and you may learn the meaning of the term tortious interference with a contract.

Wholesale/Retail offers are usually all cash, so it's easy to see how in the case of an ugly house the Realtor® gets paid from the seller's proceeds. However, if your entire wholesale and retail business revolves around buying listed houses, you'll have a tough road ahead. Here's a strong word of advice:

Your business must not depend on Realtors® to do anything.

Are Realtors® useful? Yes, in some cases, such as for buying listed junkers. But don't forget, they control the deal and you're not their only customer. This buffer (the Realtor®) between you and the seller will drive up the price and make listed houses tougher to buy.

Your best market will always be unlisted houses. The best of the best are houses the rest of the world doesn't know are for sale because they're not on the market until you plant the bug in the seller's ear you're a buyer. Here's a simple rule that separates the real players from beginners:

The easier a deal is to find, the more it costs.

Listed houses and FHA and VA repos are easy to find; therefore, they cost more, and less profit is made. It's always better to have sellers calling you, but here we'll discuss ways to find deals where you make the first contact. Stick to the FSBOs, and I promise it'll be easier to make a lot more money when you discover who wants to deal with you, which is discussed in the next chapter on prescreening.

➢ The Three Best Ways I Know To Find Ugly Houses

The first step to a successful business, any business, is to locate prospects who are predisposed to do business with you. The good thing about finding ugly houses is they're easy to spot. They just sit there and glare at you. Anyone can see they need repairs, and we assume if they're ugly, there's a reason to contact the owner to see if you can buy it at wholesale price.

Obviously, it's a numbers game. You'll buy some and some you won't. In fact, you won't get most of them, especially the ones you think ought to be the easiest to buy because they're the ugliest.

As I write this, I have just seen my Roth IRA grow $80,000 from two checks on two ugly houses I bought, rehabbed, and resold. I made $43,230 on one and $37,233 on the other—tax free for life . . . *and that was only my half!*

Both were partnered deals with people I know, so I only got half of the profits. Of course, I didn't touch the houses. In fact, I've never seen a picture of one of them! Perhaps I should go look at it. Well . . . maybe not. The check seemed to clear OK.

Ugly houses are very profitable—too profitable for you to ignore. Nonetheless, I'm hearing too many students say they'd rather do pretty houses and not mess with the uglies. But, that would be a mistake. A big mistake. Sure, pretty houses are easy in, easy out. No contractors and little or no costly entanglements. So what? Does that excuse you from harvesting the gold on the uglies? I think not! The two examples I just told you about should make my case.

You can't find pretty houses without finding ugly ones!

Turn your back if you will, but it'd be a shame to trash a couple hundred grand a year because you have blinders on. Not only that, but ugly houses are easier to find than pretties simply because they *are* ugly. Usually you find the house first and then see if the seller's needs and the existing financing make sense for you to buy. Besides, buying ugly houses requires very little communication and people skills. You don't have to meet anyone because most of the uglies are vacant, so buying is an easy process.

If rehabbing turns you off, you have several choices. You can get someone else to handle it (as I did), or you can wholesale your uglies.

Here are my best three methods for finding junkers: the

ant farm, Realtors®, and direct mail. If you implement one correctly, you should easily do a couple of deals a month. Do them all and who knows! The key word is *correctly*. Not a slap shot attempt so you can make excuses for your failure; serious people do what it takes.

*Method One: *The Ant Farm*

This is by far the most productive way to find junkers. I call it the ant farm because it involves a couple of people (ants) running around looking for ugly houses and bringing them to me. I pay $5 per lead if the leads meet my criteria of being ugly and in neighborhoods I assign.

You should be your own ant for some time. Simply drive around through low-priced neighborhoods and write down all the addresses of ugly, vacant houses. Then come home and track down the owners and call them to see if you can strike a deal. There are complete details about my ant farm in several courses—my Wholesale and Retail Cash Flow System and at our live Quick Start Real Estate School.

Here are five key points that explain where most people fail at the ant farm. Like anything else, do it right or don't whine when it doesn't work:

1. Ugly houses are in low-priced areas. You won't find them in gated communities. If you're having trouble locating them, you're in the wrong neighborhood.
2. You must look up all the addresses on the tax rolls and determine if the mailing address is different from the address of the vacant home. If so, get the phone number from Information at 411 and call the seller. No letters. Get on the phone and talk to the seller. You can usually get to your local tax rolls online by going to [*your county name.org*].
3. If you don't make contact with the seller, the rest is a waste of time. Do what you have to do to make it happen.
4. You must hire a skip tracer to find the ones you can't find. This is where most people quit, yet it's where the real money is to be made.

The harder they are to find, the bigger the profit!

I'm sick of telling people this and watching them go cheap here. If you're not going to do this, the ant farm ain't for you.

5. You must understand it's a numbers game. You can't get upset after the first 20 houses don't produce a deal.

Let's assume you send a batch of 20 houses to the skip tracer. He'll find 70 percent, or 14 sellers, which means you'll pay about $200. Suppose you get one deal out of the 14 that wholesales for a $10,000 profit. Do we need to run a spreadsheet on this? It's a no-brainer.

If you don't get a deal from the first 20 leads . . . go find 20 more!

If they don't produce, get another 20 more! Could you spend $400 to make $10,000? Why is it so difficult for sensible people to understand?

If you do what I just said, you can't fail with the ant farm unless you just totally screw up the offers. It won't fail you. Only you can fail *it*. Doesn't it stand to reason that some of the owners of the ugly houses would love to sell them to you for cash? Go find them!

*Method Two: *Realtors*®

Realtors® have always been a good source of ugly houses, even though it's been a little tougher the last couple of years to get at the deals. The real estate market has been good, which produces easier sales for the banks and brings the wannabe investors out of the woodwork. However, I've been getting listed deals all along as have many of my students. In fact, the one I mentioned earlier that made me $43,000 for my half was real estate owned (REO) by a bank and listed with a Realtor®.

Issues to consider on listed houses:

- You'll probably need some proof of funds to submit an offer. This can be the bank statement of anyone you know, a letter from a mortgage broker, a letter from anyone who says her or she will fund the deal, someone's mutual fund or IRA statement, or even your own credit card statement showing cash available to cover the purchase. Proof of funds doesn't mean the funds must come from the source of proof you provide. Just because you show a Realtor® your mother's IRA statement doesn't mean Mom is obligated to put up the money. Also remember that the only time you'll ever need proof of funds is when you use Realtors®, and not all of them will request it.

- Expect to put up a $500 deposit or more when buying listed houses.

- Keep your offers clean with no contingencies not already covered in the contract.

- You'll use the Realtor's® contract or you won't get the offer presented. Realtors® will *not* use your contract.

- The first time a Realtor® believes you can't close, game's over. The last thing you tell a Realtor® is that you want to wholesale the house. Keep your mouth shut!

- Find the ugly houses that are listed first, then call the listing agent to make an offer. Don't try to get Realtors® who deal in pretty houses to help you buy ugly ones. That's like trying to get me into a size 28 pants! It would involve excruciating pain!

*Method Three: *Direct Mail*

Direct mail will produce results if you do it correctly and stick to it. There are numerous targets to mail to, so your best bet is to pick two or three and focus on them. I'd suggest mailings to out-of-town owners of vacant, ugly houses in your own city. They're good and proven targets that yield results.

Another target is the list of condemned houses you can get from your code compliance officer. Of course, there are pre-foreclosures, probably the highest-paying segment of the business. These are easy to find because in these cases a lawsuit has been filed and is on the public record, but it's difficult to get a response from these owners. So if you're going to work pre-foreclosures, you'd better get some training.

Frankly, it takes two or three things properly implemented to get several houses a month. Don't get carried away trying to do too much. Choose your weapons and put them to work. In fact, the ant farm will be instrumental in everything I mention here. It will locate the house you buy from Realtors® and produce a list of out-of-town owners to mail to if you can't get a phone number. It's cheap and effective, and you can crank it up or slow it down as you see fit. I'd make an ant farm a part of your buying machine.

➤ *Three Good Ways To Find Pretty House Deals*

I discussed three ways to find ugly houses so it's only fitting I now cover the other side of the business. We should start with defining what a pretty house really is. It's not the price that produces the definition. The house could be high priced, but most people in the pretty house business work in the range of $70,000 to $200,000. If you're in a high-priced market such as San Francisco, where a $200,000 house is rare, your range will be higher.

The point is that pretty houses start at the bottom and go up; they're not just expensive houses, as I've noted. My definition of a pretty house is any house requiring less than $5,000 in work to get it in a good, salable condition and can be bought without paying all cash. An ugly house is one that needs rehab or a lot of repairs or even very little but it's an all-cash deal.

I'd want you to work both sides of that business and become a transaction engineer who can recognize a deal when you see it, whether it's pretty or ugly. Don't fall into the trap of trying to get so specialized that you turn your back on lots of other profits—there's gold in both ugly houses and pretty houses.

Most people start with the ugly houses, because they're easy to find and understand, and they either wholesale or rehab and retail. That's OK, but it's only a start. Pretty houses are easy in, easy out. Usually it's a "get the deed" and lease-option transaction to a tenant-buyer, which takes a few days, eliminates contractors, and reduces holding costs—plus producing a few thousand dollars in front-end profit. A person could get used to this part of the business and easily make the decision to ignore the uglies.

So how do you find pretty houses? Well, there are a number of ways, but we'll focus on three good ones here.

*Method Number One: *Signs*

Signs never fail to get calls—usually before you get home. I'm referring to stick signs you place on the side of the road. They can be put up with a pointed 1 x 2 foot stake that you can buy at Home Depot in bundles or with a wire rack.

The good news is you'll get calls. The bad news is some calls might be from the city asking you to remove one or two because someone has complained about them. If a call from the city would give you a heart attack, use other methods. Most cities have ordinances against signs, but some don't. You'll have to check into that, but the bottom line is that all cities have signs, and a lot of students elect to take their chances.

I've heard of some investors who were subjected to a fine as repeat offenders, and every once in a while I hear of a city that gets nasty. I once received a letter from a city office in Oregon asking me to advise my students that it has ordinances against these signs. So there, you've been advised.

Many students put up signs on Friday afternoon and pick them up on Sunday night to avoid aggravation from the city, which may sound foolish until you look at the numbers. The signs cost about $3 each, so if you put out 50, you've got $150 invested. Pick up the remaining 40 on Sunday night and the cost is $30 for the 10 signs that come up missing . . . and I promise, they will.

If you get 10 to 15 calls over the weekend and buy one house (as you should) with a $20,000 profit, it's a no-brainer. All of a sudden, it's worth the risk of city heat. In some areas, the city couldn't care less, and your signs have a long life. Don't be scared off by my warning here. Do your own diligence and make the best decision for you.

Most signs are on fiberboard, around 18 x 24 inches. I like black letters on yellow but have used other colors successfully. Be careful when you make up the sign; you don't want to put too much detail on it. Remember, people are moving when they see it, so make the phone number large and don't forget your Web site address if you have one set up. The signs can simply say:

I BUY HOUSES
[YOUR PHONE #]
[YOUR WEB SITE]

Don't complicate the signs and make them hard to read. You can also have your car or truck lettered with vinyl letters in bright colors. It costs about $300 for the whole job; you only pay once, the vehicle signs won't come up missing, and you shouldn't get a call from the city.

I have students doing 10 to 15 deals a year simply from their vehicle signs. Let the world know you buy houses.

*Method Two: Direct Mail Campaigns

This can be a full marketing machine all in one if you do nothing else. Not only does it work well for many people, but the list of targets is so big that you can target your chosen prospects and never run out of prospects. Even though signs work well, the best target you can hope for is an area you like. With direct mail, you use a rifle approach.

Kathy Kennebrook, student turned teacher, has developed a great course on direct mail campaigns that work well for her. She gives you all the letters, step-by-step instructions, and the results she's getting with each campaign. I'd suggest you get her stuff to make your job a lot easier. The few hundred dollars you'll spend is easily wasted in printing and postage by an untrained beginner mailing the wrong thing to the wrong list. You can contact my office for details at **800-567-6128**. By the way, she made $805,000 last year by mailing 12,000 letters throughout the year and never stuffed the first envelope. When I met Kathy, she was working as a field rep for some company paying her peanuts, spending most of her life away from home, and hating her job. You should see her now: only 4$^{1/2}$ feet tall with an income larger than most corporate CEOs.

Here's a list of some possible targets for direct mail that Kathy covers, most of which I've used and that work well for me:

- Pre-foreclosures are a gold mine if worked correctly—an entire business within the business—and are worth the time and expense to learn.
- Out-of-town owners almost always work. The list is easy to get from a Realtor® or your local records office. This is one Kathy specializes in (with a 12 percent response rate if I remember correctly). Be sure to mention the property address in the letter and include a response card to make it easy for owners to reach you without calling. Some people simply *won't* call. You must call them after they return your response card! You'll find a good sample in Appendix E.
- New homeowners who've been in their house less than two years. I've heard that more than 70 percent of foreclosures occur within the first two years of ownership, and a large percentage of those occur in the first year. Any list broker can get you the list; you'll find brokers in your yellow pages or go to **www.RonLeGrand.com/Resources**. You're looking for pretty houses so you can get the deed.
- Zip codes where you want to buy. Just pick an area, rent the list of homeowners from a list broker, and mail a postcard.
- Divorces. A sale is usually imminent, so get the list from public records and contact the owners.
- Estate sales. Mail to the trustee, who almost always needs to sell.
- FSBO (for sale by owner) ads. You can download the ads from the online classifieds in your local paper or from an FSBO magazine.
- VA (Veterans Administration) homeowners. You can get a list from a list broker and select by zip code or other factors such as property value, length of ownership, and age of the veteran.

♦ Bankruptcies are a matter of public record, and many of those filing for bankruptcy are looking to sell a home. You can pay cash for the junkers or get the deed on pretty houses and petition the bankruptcy trustee to release the house from bankruptcy.

Go to **www.RonLeGrand.com/Resources** for a national list of bankruptcies. If a seller is getting little or no money, it's usually not a problem unless the house has a lot of equity and the trustee blocks the sale, but that's the exception, not the rule. Your mail should be directed to the owner, not the trustee, and your letter should mention you specialize in bankruptcy purchases. OK, I know you don't, but you'll learn after you've done a few! You'll learn the rules, and they won't scare you anymore.

Short sales are nothing more than discounting defaulted loans on properties in foreclosure or about to be after you get the deed. My students are making huge fortunes with short sales all over America, and I'm not doing badly myself.

*Method Number Three: *Call Ads*

I know this doesn't sound appealing, but if you'll do it my way, you'll probably grow to love it. You see, I don't want you to call ads; I want you to get others to do it for you—others who'll do it because it's their job and you're paying them. It's so simple that you'll probably try to complicate it, but here it goes.

Get the Property Information Sheet from page 192 and have your helper call all of the Sunday FSBO ads every Monday night between 6 and 9 PM in areas where you want to work. Have your employee-helper fill out the basic information you need to determine if you want to call the seller back. The only info I need is the asking price, the estimated value, the loan balance, the condition of the property, the address, and whether it's listed with a Realtor®. With this information, I can prescreen the prospect sheet in five seconds and make my decision to follow up or not, as I discuss in the next chapter. If you pay your helper $5 per script, the helper will make $10 to $20 an hour, and you can avoid talking to a bunch of dead-end leads who don't want, or need, to sell.

Your job is to take the big pile of ads and reduce it to a little pile of prospects that appear motivated and willing to give you equity. That's it! You can make a few calls a week to good prospects that have been sifted and sorted out before you talk to them. This method alone could easily make you half a million a year! It's really that simple if you can recognize a deal and follow up to get it done.

➢ Twenty-Two More Ways To Find Deals

When I started, I knew that, as sure as pushing the gas pedal makes a car go faster, investing more in my buying machine would increase my income. The first several months were the toughest because I needed every dime just to keep the lights on and the roof over my head. If money is tight for you, hang in there. It *will* pay off. Think of your business as an airplane. For a plane to take off, the pilot must give it more power; the plane goes faster and faster until it finally becomes airborne. At that point, does the pilot decrease power to the engine? No! He continues to give it full throttle as the plane climbs rapidly up to cruising altitude, then its full speed ahead. Likewise, you should keep feeding fuel to your buying machine even if you're flying high, and you'll keep speeding toward your financial goals. Don't do what the so-called competition does and start cruising before you're even in the sky. Keep the buying machine cranked to full throttle.

Now let's look at the 22 more ways to find motivated sellers:

1. Credibility kit. This item is a must for every serious real estate investor. Its purpose is to identify you as someone who can be trusted. With that in mind, what do you suppose should be included?
    ♦   Presentation folder. This doesn't have to be expensive, especially if you're going to mail it out, but it should be neat and professional. You can and should spend a little more on the folders you carry in your briefcase and hand out personally as their effect on a customer will be crucial and immediate. You might even have these professionally bound at your neighborhood print shop.
    ♦   Cover letter. This is how you'll establish yourself with

someone who doesn't know you, so it's very important. It's somewhat like a résumé because it'll include personal as well as professional information, such as the number of your years in business, how long you've lived in the area, schools you've graduated from (local only), college degrees, organizations you belong to, and so on. Your credibility kit should also include either a picture of yourself or a picture of you and your family.

♦ Letters of recommendation. Get these from people who are relevant to your business. You are for instance, your closing agent and your real estate attorney. While you're at it, see if your attorney will write a letter stating that the lease-purchase agreements, lease-options, and the like are perfectly legal. A letter from your bank will also add credibility. This letter does not have to include your credit worthiness or your financial statement; a simple statement will do, such as "John Smith is a good customer in good standing with First National Bank and has been since 1999."

♦ Better business bureau membership. Join the BBB and put that in your kit. Sellers will call to check you out, and your BBB membership will go a long way toward your credibility. Being a BBB member has gotten several deals for me.

♦ Additional items. Include anything that will add to your credibility as a businessperson. References from local community leaders would be good. A letter from your insurance agent and CPA could also be included.

♦ Pictures. Finally, pictures of yourself with local celebrities make for great conversational pieces as well as more credibility reinforcement. As time goes by, you'll have more and better items to add to your kit, so never consider it finished. Once you have a good prototype, however, it's time to use it. What follows is a short list of reliable sources for motivated sellers; you'll want to use as many of these as possible. But, never stop looking for other ideas. And, don't forget to track your results.

2. Running your own ads. All investors run ads mostly online today, and many of them are the same. Your challenge is to be different without losing the simplicity and effectiveness you want. Don't be afraid to test new ideas constantly and track your results. When you get a call or email, whether from a classified ad or the other ideas I'm sharing with you,

ask where the caller saw your ad. Here are a couple of ads that work for me:

I Buy Houses
Any Condition-Price-Area
Walk Away Today - 555-5555 or Email if Online

Or how about:
I Buy Houses When Others Say No. Call 287-5244 or Email

Be innovative and try your own ideas. Run your ads in the major daily newspaper and local website, and run it 7 days a week, 365 days a year.

3. Radio spots. You can run a 30-second or a 60-second commercial. The longer format is preferable because it allows time to fully explain your program and costs roughly the same. You can get a professional station announcer to read it for you, usually for free. Then there's a long list of local sites you should place your ad and the easiest way to find them is go on Google ad type in "homes for sale in____" or "I want to buy houses in _____". You'll get a list of sites to advertise. See the resource section of this book. The cost of air time can be very affordable, about $10 to $20 per spot if you use talk radio or business stations. I don't recommend a music station because it is cost prohibitive.

4. Home shows. I'm referring to live events held in exhibit halls where you rent a booth, hand out your fliers, and talk to attendees. For better results, offer some kind of a freebie, such as a plastic visor, rule, or Frisbee with your company name on it. You can save money on these shows by hooking up with another exhibitor for just a small space to display your fliers and entry forms for your *free gift drawing*. Entry forms ask the entrant's name, address, and phone number. They give you a valuable potential lead. You might also have a questionnaire asking such things as these: Are you thinking about selling your home? Do you know anyone selling their home? Are you looking to buy a home in the near future?

5. Magnetic signs. A magnetic sign for all your vehicles is a very affordable idea. Keep it simple. For example: *I Buy Houses,*

Cash, 555-5555, and [Web site].

6.   Door hangers. A door hanger is simply a flier designed to be put on a door knob. This is a great idea for targeting a specific neighborhood where you would like to buy. On one side of the door hanger is your ad "I Buy Houses When Others Say NO," and the other side offers some kind of incentive such as free pizza. When you place the door hanger, make sure your offer is facing toward the front. Print on a bright neon-colored paper.

7.   Shirts. Have your message printed on T-shirts. You might even print it on small T-shirts for your children to wear to school. If you do this, consider printing "*My Daddy Buys Houses.*" Cute, huh?

8.   Sponsor a Little League team or bowling league. With a modest donation, you can have your company name and phone number on team uniforms and prominently display team programs—even on the playing field or bowling alley.

9.   Moving billboards. These include billboards and signs on city buses, taxi cabs, and the like, an idea I like a lot. City buses are great for targeting particular areas of town. Remember to keep your ads simple and easy to read.

10.   Bus benches. Many bus stops have park benches with space available for advertisements. Again, keep your ad simple.

11.   Golf courses. Many golf courses, both public and private, offer display advertising in various ways around each hole. Check it out.

12.   Business cards. This is another one of those obvious things. Business cards are very affordable, just remember to use both sides of the card. I like to use the back of my cards. Place business cards on bulletin boards at grocery stores or leave them at restaurants or anywhere you think people might see them.

13.   Direct mail packs. Some of the trade names are Val Pak, Money Mailer, and Paper Mint. If you use one of these, you'll

get the best response by offering a free giveaway or some kind of genuine discount, such as a free pizza or $5 off. You can have your bonus offer printed on the reverse side of your ad. Test different ideas and track your results.

14. Builders. Builders can be a great source for deals. Your lease-option offer gives them cash flow, top dollar. Don't ignore this idea.

15. Corporate communications. Many large companies have their own in-house newsletter and/or bulletin boards. These are good places to reach employees who are being transferred out, laid off, divorced, or undergoing other lifestyle changes that require them to sell.

16. Tax rolls. You can locate and access property owners who are out of town through tax rolls. Mail owners a letter along with your credibility kit. Don't do just one mailing either. Mail them at least five times, each time about three weeks apart. Track your records.

17. Ads in FSBO magazines. This is a great place to run your ad that reads, "I Buy or Lease Houses." If you're cold-calling as I mentioned earlier, you can reference your ad when you cold-call sellers from the magazine.

18. Foreclosure service. This is a service that provides you with the names and addresses of people in your county who are in foreclosure. This by itself can be a very lucrative market. It does require a special kind of knowledge, but it is easy to learn and well worth doing.

19. Vacant houses. Great place to leave a flier or business card. You may try direct mailing along with your credibility kit. If the residents have left a forwarding address, the post office will deliver a solution to a problem they may be looking to solve.

20. Ads in homeowner association newsletters. Most neighborhood homeowners associations have newsletters and welcome advertisers. These newsletters are mailed to every homeowner in a particular neighborhood. The ads are

cheap, so you can afford to keep your ad there forever. When you have a house to sell in that neighborhood, why not advertise it for sale there also?

21. Yellow pages. Some of my best leads used to come from a dollar-bill-sized ad under Real Estate in the yellow pages. Today it's **YP.com** and **YELP.com** and numerous other local sites you can Google. You won't get a lot of calls, but those you do seem to be of good quality, and this seems to be the result my students report. The downside is it's a yearlong commitment of several hundred dollars a month, so probably not the place for a beginner to start.

22. Real estate agents (continued). When you're dealing with real estate agents, keep in mind they aren't in business to make money for you. They are in the business to make money for themselves. So you need to approach them with a game plan outlining the several ways they will make money by helping you find deals.

I target small independent real estate offices and the top listing agents with big-name firms. I tell them the kinds of properties I'm interested in buying, what I expect from our relationship, and what they can expect from me. My goal (and yours) is to develop a working relationship with an agent that will be profitable for both of you.

It's important to show real estate agents that you're professional and serious about buying a lot of properties. Show them your credibility kit. Explain that money is not a problem, that you can close fast, and you rarely have contingencies. If meetings go well, arrange future meetings at regular times when you'll exchange information. Agents will give you the new properties they've found, and you will bring them up-to-date on the progress you've made with each property they've previously given you. Don't depend on only one or two agents, however, always be on the lookout for new agents to work with.

More on Real Estate Agents
The following is what I want agents to do for me and what I will do for them:

◆ Find properties that can't get listed. The listing agent gets a commission even if another agent or agency sells the house. For that reason, real estate agents are always looking for properties to list. In their search, they may run across sellers who can't list because they have no equity and can't afford to pay commissions. I ask them to simply refer me to these sellers. If I'm able to put together a deal, I'll pay $500 as a referral fee. I choose $500 because it's enough to get their attention and make it worth their while. Sometimes their fee will be higher if the deal has a lot of equity.

♦ Find sellers that are in pre-foreclosure. Most real estate agents aren't interested in a property in pre-foreclosure because of time pressure—but I am. If they refer these properties to me and I'm able to put together a deal, I will again pay them a $500 finder's fee. In some cases, where it makes sense, agents will make $500 and also make the commission if they find a buyer first.

♦ Find vacant properties in nice neighborhoods. Vacant, unlisted properties usually represent a problem you can solve at a profit. The property may be vacant for any number of reasons, including pre-foreclosure, a divorce, transfer, and so on. There is no way for agents to make money on a vacant house unless they can find the seller and get the listing. The effort is usually not worth agents' time, so I ask them to give me addresses and other particulars. If I can put together a deal, I'll pay them my $500 finder's fee. What could be easier?

♦ Find cheap, ugly properties listed below market value and in need of repairs. Granted, it may be a little difficult finding a good real estate agent who'll continue to find you these properties. They know most of your offers won't be accepted, and those that are will be low offers that pay only small commissions. However, if you haven't limited agents to just cheap properties, they'll be glad to find these for you because it is one of the several ways they can make money working for you.

♦ Bring me any deal that might be profitable, where the seller is motivated and open to terms. This could lead me to get the deed or owner financing deals as long as it's not listed yet and a full commission is not expected. The deal will determine how I pay my agent. When you're just beginning your relationship, you may want to pay agents a little more. Remember, if an agent didn't bring you the deal, you wouldn't have made the profit. So, why should I mind paying agents? I don't!

Another benefit I offer real estate agents is to refer buyers to them—that is, people who have called me about houses I have advertised but, for some reason or another, didn't want the property. This potential benefit gives an agent a strong incentive to work hard at finding deals for me. If you work hard to make money for your agents, they'll work hard for you. If they don't, find other agents.

"No man ever achieved worthwhile success who did not, at one time or other, find himself with at least one foot hanging well over the brink of failure."

Napoleon Hill

Dear Ron,

I've been studying Creative Real Estate for a long time and have courses from all of the big GURUS except yours until this last Thursday.

You might say I'm "course poor". Until recently I worked full time at a 60 hr a week job. I philandered through them all looking for the just the right system to get involved in once I retired. Problem was I didn't want to work hard. I already did that years and years... and I didn't want to take risks on real estate that, to me, sounded more like schemes, than deals. I'm so glad I took this course!!

As a result of this two day TERMS event, I have become a convert. I've absolutely found what I've been looking for. A great business, I can run without a lot of work, make a lot of money including passive income, with a built in trained team and mentors which minimize as much as possible the chances for failure. What more could and investor want???

Thank you, Ron for putting on such a great event and more importantly figuring out the system and being willing to share it with us!

Sincerely,

Lill Gravatt

Chapter 8
Step 2 - Prescreening Prospects

This may very well be the most important chapter in this entire book because the ability to tell the difference between a deal and a dud is the difference between success and failure. It's also the only way you can ever implement my credo: *"The Less I Do, the More I Make."*

Some investors spend their time driving around looking at dozens of properties a month, even hundreds. This is not only a gross waste of time but it's downright stupid. Chasing dead-end leads is similar to dealing with unmotivated sellers and can be a tremendous waste of time, and energy. Unfortunately, many people never really learn how to avoid it. Well, I can solve this problem very simply: *prequalify every prospect that comes your way.*

I've found if you spend as little as five minutes getting prequalifying information from a prospect, you may avoid spending hours and hours gathering details about a property you never had a chance of buying. And any time you can spend minutes to save hours, it's like putting money in the bank.

Some investors have a tendency to take a phone call from a prospect and rush right out to look at a house in hopes something will develop—especially if business has been slow. They'll be out there measuring for carpet and gathering useless facts before they even know if they have a chance to put the house under contract. What a crazy waste of time, especially when you know you should never leave your desk without a solid reason.

Properly prequalifying a prospect helps you determine if further action is warranted. When making the initial contact with a prospect, you should ask yourself these three questions to determine where you can make the deal:

1. *Can I buy the house wholesale?*
2. *Can I create a "subject-to" deal?*
3. *Can I option or lease-option the house?*

If the situation doesn't result in a positive yes answer to one of these three questions, you don't have a deal. It's that simple. There is no reason for you to waste any further time on the conversation, much less travel across town to look at a house you'll never own.

Five minutes is all it should take to determine if you can create a deal with a prospective seller. Of course, you'll have to take the seller's word on things like the condition of the house, mortgage balances, liens, judgments, and so on. However, if the information seems reliable, and you feel the seller is motivated to pursue one of the money-producing models stemming from the three questions presented above, then you should arrange a meeting to verify your assumptions about the viability of the deal.

When I leave my desk, my chances of putting a house under contract are about 80 percent. By the time I ease the Mercedes out of the driveway, I've fully qualified my prospect, and I know I won't be just collecting a lot of useless facts.

Instead of being professional fact finders, we should get into the business of being professional offer makers. If you follow this prequalifying procedure on every lead, you'll save yourself a lot of wasted, unproductive hours, and you'll start to find the business really coming together for you.

➢ Prescreening Junkers

This is really a simple matter of math after you've collected four key items:

1. **After repair value (ARV)**
2. **Asking price**
3. **Loan balance**
4. **Estimated repair costs**

I'll give you a magic formula to use when buying ugly houses that took me ten years to create, and then I'll cover the four key items above. This formula will never fail you no matter where you live or what price the house you buy; it works in any city. If you stick to it, buying junkers is easy. If you sway from it and use the SWAG theory (scientific wild ass guess), it'll be only a matter of time before your next seminar from Hard Knocks University.

Here's the magic formula when making all-cash offers only:

ARV x 70% - Repairs = MAO

That's after repair value (ARV) times 70 percent minus total repair estimate equals maximum allowable offer (MAO). However, MAO is not what you'll pay. Your offer should always be at least $5,000 below MAO, or don't buy the house. If you do, you'll pay too much; that's not a guess, its simple math.

Forgoing a long drawn-out explanation of what went into the creation of my formula, here's the simple realty. Your net profit should be at least 20 percent of the sales price if you were to buy, fix up, and sell. Your other costs will eat up another 10 to 15 percent, which is at least 30 percent off the top for expenses and profit, not including repairs.

Using the 30 percent number automatically adjusts the dollars as the value of the house goes up or down, although the percentages won't change. However, the cost of repairs is considered case-by-case, varying with every deal, so you can't put a percentage number in a formula that's reliable.

So ARV times 70 percent means you've taken 30 percent off the top for profit and costs except for repairs. That ensures at least 20 percent going to the net column, so you factor in your *minimum* profit before you make an offer.

If you intend to wholesale this house to an investor, you can expect him or her to pay at or about MAO for the house. Don't expect the investor to pay more; you must leave enough of a reason for the investor to want your house. So if you intend to sell at MAO, you must buy the house more cheaply so you build in a profit for yourself of at least $5,000. The further below MAO you can buy, the bigger your wholesale profit.

You may be wondering how you can buy a house this far below ARV. The answer is simple: It must be ugly (filthy, stinking ugly) the kind of ugly that repulses most people. A lot of rotten wood, termite damage, leaking roofs, overgrown shrubs and lawns, rats, roaches, dead animals, toilets overflowing with human feces, and on and on. The house should smell so bad when you open the front door that the odor drives you backward.

The uglier the house, the bigger the profit.

Houses you can fix over a weekend with a little sweat and a paintbrush are usually not the kind you can buy below MAO. *You'll spin your wheels on the wrong prospects if you miss this point and get no offers accepted.*

The next most important item when prescreening ugly houses to determine whether they're prospects worth chasing or instantly passed over is this:

There must be a big spread between the ARV and asking price or the deal is dead.

➤ An Important Prescreening Lesson

Whether you're buying a pretty house or an ugly one, there is one universal truth you must never violate or you're a goner. This is a principle that many do violate in their early days of investing, most of them messing up and growing to hate real estate—even though real estate investing wasn't the problem. The real problem was the investor who didn't take time to learn this principle:

Never buy a property unless you can get free equity the day you buy it or know how to create free equity shortly thereafter.

People who pay retail price for real estate don't understand this rule and usually live in the property. They're not in it for the money, but you are. Your profit can come only from free equity in the quick turn business. You must get it with the deal or you shouldn't buy the house. That's why a house where the seller is asking at or about ARV is not a house worth chasing.

It's a dead horse, so bury it now; you can't motivate an unmotivated seller. Move on quickly and find the people who want to deal with you.

Whether it's a pretty house or an ugly house, your objective is to find sellers who *need* to sell, not *want* to sell.

Sellers who need to sell will make you rich. Sellers who want to sell will make you old, and tired and will put you out of business.

Find the people who want to deal with you and lose the rest at lightning speed. If you do, you should succeed; if you don't, you'll most certainly fail. I've been at this for well over 30 years, 3,000 houses, and over 500,000 students. Not one thing creates failure more than trying to deal with the wrong people. It can only lead to rejection, discouragement, and failure.

And that's why the *spread* is the big key when processing whether a junker is a prospect. The bigger the spread, the better the prospect. That's also why the ugliest of houses are usually the ones with the biggest spread. The seller is more motivated, therefore driving down the asking price and increasing the gap between the after repair value and the asking price.

Many times you'll discover the asking is close to, or even below, MAO. When this happens, you have a hot prospect, and nothing should stop you from coming to terms. This usually occurs on only the *really* ugly houses.

Now, let's discuss how to find the ARV and estimate repairs. Before we do, remember you must know the ARV, the asking price, the loan balance, and needed repairs before you can make an offer. Never make an offer before you find out what a seller wants. If you let sellers speak first, you may discover they'll take less than you're willing to pay. You speak first, and you'll never get lower. You instantly lost the negotiating process.

What comes out of your mouth will determine what goes into your bank account.

You must know the loan balance, and the only way to

know is to ask. If a seller owes more than the amount you're willing to pay, a cash offer is out of the question—unless it's in default and you understand short sales. For you to not know what's owed but then to make an offer for less makes you look foolish and may end the relationship.

Knowing the loan balance instantly tells us whether this deal is a good prospect or is better suited for a "subject-to" deal (get the deed). Many times you can get a house for free by simply taking over the debt and putting up no cash but still get a lot of equity because the house needs repairs.

Here's an example of one I did recently. The house was worth $115,000 after repairs. The dad had died and left the son the house with a $52,000 mortgage and needing $15,000 in repairs. Of course, that looked like $30,000 to the untrained seller, who was a pharmacist. The seller called on the basis of our ad and said he just wanted out. He was sick of the house after devoting several weekends to it and had simply lost interest. We went to the house, met the seller, got the deed, and left owning the house. The seller even agreed to make the next three payments simply because we asked.

We spent $15,000 on repairs and cashed out at $114,900. Not bad for a free ugly house, huh?

How to Determine the ARV (After Repair Value)
These are several ways you can make a determination of the ARV:

- ◆ You're licensed and have access to the Multiple Listing Service (MLS).
- ◆ You know or will find a real estate agent who can do a market analysis for you. Because you'll be making offers on some listed houses, the listing agent should provide the after repair value (ARV) on these. This can also lead to a relationship that allows you to find comparable sales completed on non-listed houses.
- ◆ You subscribe to a database service that allows you to tap into tax rolls so you can pull up your own market analysis. You should investigate a service of this type in your area. We use First American Real Estate Solutions, which you can

locate on the Internet and is also referred to as Win 2 Data.

♦ Look for similar houses in good condition on the market in the subject area. Call agents and FSBOs (houses for sale by the owner) from yard signs to determine asking prices.

♦ If you're contacting the seller directly, you should always ask what he or she thinks the house would be worth if it were in excellent condition. This may or may not be a real number, but it's something to go by until you can do a more diligent investigation. Always ask how the seller arrived at the value. If it came from an agent's analysis or an appraisal, remember that it's probably the "as is" value if the house is ugly. You're looking for the after repair value, so it should be higher. If the seller's figures came from the tax assessment, it's usually well below the real market value.

♦ There are numerous web sites you can go to for comps (see Resources). Type in search words like "comparable market value" or "comps" or "real estate value," and you'll get plenty to choose from. Some charge and some are free.

Estimating Repairs

This one scares most people with no background in repairs. I guess we should be glad it does, because the public's lack of knowledge in this area is what creates the opportunity in junkers. Most people think it costs twice what it really does to repair a house. It won't take long to get a handle on this; in fact, it's one of the easiest things to learn if you realize you don't have to be that close to make a deal work—all you have to do is get in the ballpark.

I've renovated between 600 and 700 houses, and here's a shocker for you:

I have never been correct on my repair estimates—not even once.

Repairs always cost more or less than I anticipated, usually more. But, it never killed the deal or caused me to lose money. I've always made a handsome profit on every rehab. You see, if you use the MAO formula I gave you, there's a margin for error already built in. Besides, it's your buyer's opinion of repairs that counts, not yours, if you intend to wholesale the house. Usually, wholesale buyers underestimate repairs anyway, so you can be way off and still wholesale the house.

If your repair estimate seems to kill your deal, the problem isn't your estimate. The real problem is that you got away from my formula, used SWAG (scientific wild ass guess) and paid too much. Once that happens, it's downhill the rest of the way. Pay too much and there's not much you can do to make it up. Buy it right, and you can mess up everything afterward and still make a profit.

But don't worry, I'll make it easy for you to estimate repairs; you'll soon be doing it by walking around a house or looking at photos as I do. Here's my simple system. Most houses you find to wholesale or retail will be in the lower end of the market, ranging from 1,000 to 2,000 square feet and one or two stories. After a while, they all start to look alike. Your renovation costs will run between $10,000 and $25,000 on these houses 95 percent of the time. So, the system for estimating becomes simple:

Your repair cost will be $10,000, $15,000, $20,000, or $25,000. . . pick one.

Yep! It's that simple. Just trust your instincts, and you'll be in the ballpark with an estimate that's good enough to arrive at a repair cost for making an offer. But what if you're wrong? In fact, I'll guarantee you're wrong. So what? If you're wholesaling, it won't matter. If you were retailing, I'd expect you to get a "real" estimate from a contractor or two before you close the purchase. If you're too far off, you can change your offer, back out, or wholesale the house. It doesn't matter.

Of course, if you are one of those analytical personalities, you'll ignore my suggestion and dot every "I" and cross every "t" before you can make a decision. While you're doing all that and warming up your repair software program, my trained students and I will have made an offer, gotten it accepted, sold the house, cashed the check, and spent the money. But, hey, at least you'll feel good about your repair estimate on a house you'll never buy.

➤ *Ugly House Exit Strategies*

Most investors buy ugly houses to either wholesale quickly or rehab and retail to an owner-occupant. Some investors keep them for rentals after rehabbing, but I don't like this plan because it involves long-term debt to raise the money to buy and repair, requiring a payment low enough for a positive cash flow. This debt is usually personally guaranteed—a cardinal sin to me. There are other, much better ways to buy keepers. The most common is just getting the deal on not-so-ugly houses and taking over non-personally guaranteed debt.

Whether you intend to wholesale, retail, or rent, the buying process is the same on ugly houses. Your exit doesn't change the MAO formula *if you're paying cash.* If you're new to the business, I'd strongly suggest you stick to wholesaling and get some checks before venturing into the world of rehabbing and contractors. For that reason, I won't be covering that part of the business in this book, but it's covered in my Wholesale and Retail Cash Flow System you get on my web site at **www.RonsWholesaleCourse.com**. In fact, it took an all-day seminar on six CDs to cover from the time you purchase to the time you sell; I can't do the subject justice in a book aimed at exposing you to the whole business.

Now let's move into the world of prescreening pretty houses to see how we can make some more fast money without rehabbing.

➤ **Prescreening Pretty Houses**

There's no MAO formula that applies to pretty houses, but the rule about getting free equity stands. If you can't get free equity, why would you want the house? Fortunately, you don't have to have a lot of equity to make quick easy money. Because you don't have to raise cash to buy a house or repair it, you can operate with less equity and costly entanglements. However, the same principle applies to the spread between the ARV and the asking price. Whether a house is pretty or ugly, the best prospects are those with the most free equity.

The bad news is that most people who call you to sell

their pretty house will want close to the ARV. They are not prospects—they're "suspects." You can't work with them, and you should know it immediately on learning the ARV and the asking price are close. Remember, you can't make unmotivated sellers motivated—they either need to sell or they don't.

The good news is that some sellers who call are willing to give up a substantial amount of equity in exchange for debt relief and peace of mind. You'll know it as soon as you ask their opinion of the market value and the ARV, and then ask what they want. If the spread is big, you may have a prospect that needs to sell.

How big is *big?*

Good question! The answer depends on your knowledge of your planned exit strategy and your personal financial situation. Here are your choices of exit strategies on pretty houses that you lease-option from a seller or you get the deed:

♦ Immediately install a lease-option tenant-buyer and get a nonrefundable option deposit of at least 3 percent of the ARV. This is the most common and most profitable exit and also the easiest and quickest.
♦ Sell for cash to a qualified buyer.
♦ Move in yourself.

If you choose to sell with a lease-option, your monthly payments on the "subject-to" debt you took over must be low enough to be covered by the incoming rent, or this choice is not available. (The same applies if you lease-option from the seller.) Therefore, your only choice is to cash out now if the payment is high. In that case, you'll want more equity so you can make a decent profit; the minimum should be 20 percent of the sales price.

You can live with less equity if the payment is low because you can lease-option the house to a tenant-buyer quickly and pick up several thousand dollars from the option deposit. I'd suggest you get at least 10 percent of the value in *free* equity before considering to take the house. Too many deals are out there to take less. Here's an example to help you understand this a little better.

A seller calls you with a three-bedroom, two-bath house (a 3/2) in good condition worth $150,000. She owes $138,000, and the loan is current. On asking her the magic words, "Will you sell the house for what you owe on it?" you learn all she wants is debt relief and a quick exit. Her monthly payment is $1,182, which includes taxes and insurances. You figure it would rent for at least $1,200 a month and maybe more. Armed with this information you collected in just a few minutes, the best plan is to get the deed, immediately put a lease-option tenant in the house for about $159,000, and get a $5,000 to $10,000 option deposit within a few days. You didn't get a lot of equity, but you'll make a quick $5,000 to $10,000 up front and still have a back-end payday if your tenant gets financing to buy in the future. The payment is covered by rent, and you acquired a nice asset with no money or credit at risk while at the same time helping out the seller. She got her life back, you got a house, and your tenant-buyer got a home.

The deal I just described is common and widely available in your city. I'll bet there's one waiting for you within a mile or two from where you live. Even if the numbers are different, the technique is the same.

This deal would work the same way whether you got the deed or you lease-optioned from the seller. The exit is still to lease-option to a tenant-buyer, made possible because you got some free equity and took over a reasonable monthly payment that could be covered by rent. Even if you want to move in to the house yourself, you'll want a reasonable monthly payment and some free equity.

If you intend to option the house and resell it without the right to install a tenant-buyer, *free equity is the ruling factor* the more you can get, the more you'll want the deal. I'd suggest at least 20 percent, and I'd work hard to get more.

Earlier I mentioned my student Marco, who made $2,450,000 on one house. He did this by optioning an $8,500,000 house for $4,000,000 with a $100 deposit and selling it at auction

43 days later for $5,600,000. He also sold some furnishings and a yacht belonging to the same seller and got a percentage of these items. (This house had been listed with a Realtor® for four years with no sale.) Marco moved it in 43 days. And some people think the cost of education is expensive—ignorance costs a lot more.

The point here is that on luxury homes you must get a much bigger spread than 20 percent. Most of the time you'll be selling well below market to move a house quickly, so don't back yourself into a corner by agreeing to pay too much.

Any time you deal in houses above the $300,000 range, a 20 percent spread in most markets doesn't excite me. After all, a Realtor® and closing costs would eat up 10 percent. A seller who won't give up a lot of so-called equity is a seller who *wants* to sell, not *needs* to sell. Move on.

The *loan balance* is another key element in prescreening. A good sign the seller needs debt relief more than cash to sell is when the asking price and the loan are not far apart. If the loan and the asking price are far apart, on the other hand, the seller is looking for cash and debt relief.

Good news: Most of the houses you lease-option or get the deed for will be for the loan amount or sometimes a little cash to move. This type of deal will make up 80 to 90 percent of your pretty house deals and are easy to find.

This week I have purchased two houses "subject-to." The first house is in excellent condition and is worth $185,000. The seller owes $142,000 with a payment of $1,165 a month. He was asking $10,000 but accepted $2,000 and deeded me the house. That's $43,000 of free equity for $2,000. You don't need a computer to figure this is a good deal. The second house is worth $95,000 and needs about $3,000 in clean-up work. The seller owes $62,000 and wanted no money because she was behind two payments of $485. I got the deed and will make up the payments as soon as I lease-option the house to a tenant-buyer. I'll do so "as is" on a work for equity program and let the buyer do the repairs in exchange for a little equity. I expect to sell the house for $90,000 "as is" with a minimum deposit of $3,000 from the buyer from which I'll make up the payments. That's

$28,000 in free equity that cost me nothing.

To me this deal is barely worth doing. To you it may be a home run, especially if it's your first deal.

"Dealing with unmotivated sellers is like kissing a toad with warts. . . it'll give you a bad taste for toads."

Ron LeGrand®

Brian & Kristine Lambrecht- Lake Orion, MI

Greetings Ron, Ray and gang!

When we bought your course and boot camp from a real estate convention here in Michigan, we immediately started listening to your many CD's. We had a house that we were lease optioning to a tenant, they had to relocate in August and so the home needed a NEW optionee. The prior residents were supposed to buy it for $152,000–we figured we would increase the price to $159,900–but on your CD (which the timing of when we listened to that particular one couldn't have been better!), you said to make sure we "research" market values BEFORE we put a price on a home–not to assume we are experts at knowing our market!! Thank goodness we took that tip to heart. Because we took the extra few hours to drive the neighborhood and get a CMA done by an agent friend, we ended up asking $168,900 on a "No Bank Qualifying" ad (attached) and had a family MOVE IN within 2 weeks of the ad! (They actually moved in the day after the other residents moved out!) The new optionees gave me a $5000 option fee (the prior residents had forfeited $4000), and are paying an extra $50/month over what the prior residents paid. They agreed to the $165,900 without hesitation!!!That GREAT tip paid for our Millionaire Maker Boot camp, alone (and then some!!)! It proves that knowledge IS power and NEVER stop learning!!

We can't wait to get our really "huge" deal, so we can apply part of those proceeds to the MIS boot camp– we were one number away from winning it for free at the Millionaire boot camp–we were crushed when the last number was not ours–but we will get there, and soon!! I hope the guy that won realizes what a truly wonderful, prosperous gift he received!!

Congratulations on your book and show–Best of luck on both!!

Brian and Kristine Lambrecht

Brian & Kristine Lambrecht- Lake Orion, MI

Happy Holidays Ron, Ray and gang!

A motivated seller called us on our "Home Debt Relief" ad (i.e. We buy/lease houses, make your payments, etc.). We lease optioned her home for $144,000 (market value $155,000), 3.5 year term, making her mortgage (PITI) payments of $1042/month, zero down, and we do not start taking over her payments for 3 months! After 45 days of advertising (cold, snow, Christmas–aaaahhhh!!), we have finally found a great family who will be lease optioning the home from us as follows: $165,900 on a 2 year lease option, $4000 down, $1095/month with no rental credit!! Yeah!! It does feel wonderful (and safe) getting in with nothing down in addition to get one month of "free" rental income to boot! The $500 deposit check is above and the remainder of the $4000 option fee plus 1st month's

rent will come before we hand over the keys and sign the final contracts next week!

Thank you,

Brian and Kristine Lambrecht

Single Family, Lake Orion, MI
Price: $165,900 on a 2 yr Lease-to-Own term

Chapter 9
Step 3 - Constructing And Presenting Offers

There are only two types of houses on which you can construct and present offers: pretty houses and ugly houses. If you'll remember, most pretty house offers involve getting the deed, an option, or a lease-option. Most wholesale/retail offers are simple all-cash offers.

In the last chapter I covered the process of constructing offers, but I'll do a quick recap before I get into using a few magic words for talks with sellers. Wholesale/retail offers are easy to construct. Find the ARV, estimate repairs quickly, ask if there's a loan balance, and apply the MAO formula:

ARV x 70% - Repairs = MAO

Now, back off the MAO by at least $5,000—more if it's really ugly or in a war zone. No science, all math.

Pretty house offers are also easy to construct once you understand your objective is to get the deed for little or no money, lease-option for little or no money, or option.

All require free equity or it's a no go. Try to get in with little or no money, and don't guarantee debt. Make sure you're dealing with sellers who need to sell and you'll find all of this much easier than you think. This advice covers 75 percent of the deals you do. The rest can be covered in our training and really can't be done here without causing you more harm than good.

➢ Magic Words That Make Millions For The Real Estate Entrepreneur

I've just finished reading (for the second time) a book called *Magic Words That Bring You Riches,* authored by my good friend Ted Nicholas. Ted has sold over $200 million of information products worldwide by direct marketing. Over the years he put together a collection of "magic words" to persuade people to do things they ordinarily wouldn't do.

In *Magic Words,* Ted discusses how to do such things as get the best table in a restaurant and first-class seats on airplanes. He talks about how to slash the cost of a room at first-class hotels and attract all the money you need for any business venture. Want to approach a member of the opposite sex and immediately elicit interest? How about renting a Mercedes for the price of a Ford or buying jewelry at below wholesale prices?

Ted can tell you how to attract the best employees to make your business prosper, as well as how to get capable people to work for free. He even discusses ways to gain financial interests in other people's companies without investing one red cent. Pretty cool stuff, huh? And that's just the first few chapters. This book is also a masterful direct marketing bible covering every aspect of the business by a consummate professional. As I said, I read it twice.

Then it hit me! Like Ted, I've got a collection of magic words I've accumulated over the years, most designed to help me get into or out of a real estate deal. All of them work. The words you are about to read have made me millions of dollars and, if used properly, could do the same for you. The truth is that students have been trying to get me to do this for years, but it was Ted Nicholas's book that pulled the trigger.

Here's a set of magic words you should use daily to buy junkers:

"If I pay you all cash and close quickly, what's the least you would accept?"

And that's always followed by:

"Is that the best you can do?"

These words cut to the chase and save you a lot of time otherwise spent beating around the bush. Of course, if you're naming the price you'll pay before you ask what the seller wants, I'll have to take you out behind the woodshed.

Ye who speaks first have big mouth and will pay handsome price for house.

Those words aren't exactly magic, but they speak the truth nonetheless. Never, *never* name the price you'll pay or the down payment or monthly payment you'll pay or accept when selling. OK, let's say you've asked, "Is that the best you can do?" and the seller says yes. A good follow-up line that works for me is:

> *"So you're saying if I don't give you $_____, you won't sell the house?"*

Now if the answer is still yes, you won't be buying today unless you're willing to change the focus to a terms deal rather than a price deal.

A good icebreaker to use when you want to make it clear that you're not happy with the number you've been quoted is:

> *"What's your second choice?"*

I usually chuckle or use a hint of humor when I ask this. It's better than simply saying "I won't pay the asking price."

Let's say you're trying to get a seller to name the asking price and the seller just won't. You know better than to pressure, but you can't get the seller to break. Try this:

> *"How about a dollar?"*

This will get through and probably produce an answer. If so, you're back in the screening process and know where you stand. If not, you can come back with this:

> *"I simply have too many prospects to work with to waste time on those I can't buy. If you'll tell me what you're asking, I'll know quickly if we can do business. Is that fair?"*

By this time, the seller's usually in or out. You can't buy houses from uncooperative sellers. By the way, did you notice some powerful magic words hidden in there? Take note of how I tend to answer a question with a question. "Is that fair?" turned my response into a question and put the responsibility to answer back on the seller. It also softened the blow and made me seem warmer and fuzzier. "Is that fair?" is a powerful set of magic words that should become a part of your everyday vocabulary with almost everything you negotiate.

Let's say you're prescreening a seller who has a house with a mortgage balance. First, you want to know what's owed on the property or you can't possibly determine whether it's a deal. These aren't magic words, but they are critical ones:

"*What do you owe on the house?*"

What if the seller responds that it's none of your business? You then say:

"*I buy _____ houses per year and use many different methods. I'm probably the most serious buyer you've talked to yet. However, I'll need the facts to be able to present you with an intelligent offer. Will this be a problem for you?*"

Again, a question in an answer's clothing. Did I not sock it to them on that one? Frankly, anyone who won't give you the facts is not ready to sell yet. You got your answer. . . move on. You can't make unmotivated sellers motivated.

Now you have your answer. You know the loan balance. Now it's time to find out where you're headed with this deal, so ask:

"*Will you sell the house for what you owe on it?*"

Those magic words can make you $500,000 a year if you ask them on all your deals. With just those 12 little words, you'll know instantly whether you'll be getting a free house by taking over the debt or an almost-free house with debt plus a little cash thrown in. Of course, you may also learn that the seller wants full price and isn't flexible. Again, you found out what you needed to know with 12 words. Now you know whether to proceed with the deal or move on.

Now let's say you can't get a deed because of the due-on-sale clause or the seller won't trust you with his or her credit. But you see opportunity there and a lease-option makes sense. Here's the opening line for presenting the offer:

> *"I will lease your house with the right to buy it for the loan balance when I purchase. I'll guarantee your payment and maintenance until the loan is paid off and the house is out of your life. How does that sound?"*

Notice how all the benefits come before the question. The seller has enough information to encourage a positive response. Isn't that better than asking "Will you lease-option your home to me?" Another good question that will ease the seller's mind and make you seem genuine is this:

> *"If it doesn't work for both of us, then we don't want to do it, do we?"*

That makes it pretty clear that you're not desperate to make the deal. Another version is:

> *"If this will cause you to lose sleep at night, I'd rather not do it. Is it going to be a problem?"*

Here's a good one to break a stalemate and get you back in negotiation, as well as collect more facts that might lead to different offers:

> *"If you and I can't do business today, what will you do with the house?"*

This also gets the seller thinking particularly about all the ugly answers to that question. The answer may be:

> "I'll put it on the market or list with a Realtor® until it sells."

Your response:

> *"And what if it doesn't sell?"*

At least you'll get a feel for whether this seller is worthy of your follow-up list. I hope you know by now that . . .

All sellers' minds will change with time and circumstance.

Here's one you'll love if you're a beginner and worried about the seller finding out that you don't exactly know what you're doing. First, don't sweat it. You don't have to appear to be an expert. You can try to fake it, but if you're confronting intelligent sellers, many times they'll see through you and try to ask you embarrassing questions. So if you're asked if you've ever done this before, use these words:

> *"Well actually, no. This is my first deal after graduating from some rather intense training. I was hoping you'd help me do it right. "*

Asking for help brings you down to the seller's skill level and you've built trust by answering truthfully. Don't worry about the seller's expecting you to be an expert. If you seem sincere and excited, you'll usually get the deal. In fact, being too smart or seeming too confident will often turn off more people than if you appear to be a novice. They'll think you're too green to cheat them.

Now let's say you're talking to a seller about carrying a mortgage and the subject of interest comes up. Your goal is zero interest, so you shouldn't be the one to initiate conversation on this topic. If the seller doesn't mention interest, you shouldn't either.

When presenting an installment offer, the magic words are:

> *"I'll pay $_____ per month until you're paid in full."*

Of course, this means you've divided the loan amount by the monthly principal payment you want to pay, excluding interest. If the seller comes back with "What interest rate is that?" your response is:

> *"Why do you need interest?"*

Then if you get more argument and it becomes a sticking issue, you could respond by saying:

> *"What's more important—getting interest or the house being sold now?"*

If that doesn't get the job done, say:

> *"If I give you interest, how much can we lower the price?"*

Or: *"Will you sell to me with no down payment?"*

Or: *"Would you wait six months (or a year) for your first payment?"*

Or: *"Would you take 25 percent off the balance I owe you if I agree to pay you off within _____ years?"*

Of course, these same tactics can be used if the seller is asking you to raise your offer. You'll notice it all comes down to some very powerful magic words that can be adapted to many uses (If I . . . Would you . . .).

Here are some magic words that you can use when optioning a house:

> *"If we can agree on a price I will option your house and use all my resources to get it sold. All I need is a key to show it and a written option agreement to get started. Is that fair?"*

If the seller balks or starts coming up with objections you can defuse them with this:

> *"Mr. Seller, I'm spending my money and my time on getting this house sold, and if I don't succeed, I lose not you."*

Obviously, these aren't all the magic words you can use, and they don't cover every possible use, but I'll tell you from experience that they're worth a fortune if you use them.

➢ *Presenting Offers*

Dealing with a FSBO is a simple matter of coming to an oral agreement and then converting it to writing with a purchase and sale (P&S) agreement, a lease-option agreement, an option agreement, or an actual deed transferring ownership on the spot. Until you have a written agreement, you have nothing but words. An oral agreement "ain't" worth the paper it's written on. Get it in writing quickly.

Use a P&S agreement when a formal closing will take place later, such as in an all—cash purchase. Usually a lease-option, an option, and a deed transfer are done on the spot with a tabletop closing in the seller's kitchen. Some get a P&S agreement and have the seller meet at an attorney's office within a few days to have the documents signed. I prefer you do the latter but will admit hundreds of tabletop closings are done daily all over the country.

A good practice is to get all the paperwork you think you'd possibly need signed ASAP. You can always have them re-signed in front of an attorney later. Get a commitment while the seller is willing and ready. Postponing that commitment might give your competition a window of opportunity.

If this process scares you, I understand. In the beginning it's scary walking into someone's home with a file folder and leaving as the owner of the home. It defies all your senses and previous training. It shouldn't be that easy. Why would people leave a loan in their name and trust you with their credit and just give you a house with free equity?

That's a hard one to grasp while you're reading a book, but the first time you go to see a seller who *needs* to get out now, you'll begin to understand that all the stuff that bothers you isn't bothering the seller. Remember this:

It's not your job to think for other people. It's your job to give them choices and let them decide what's best for themselves.

If your prospects have been prescreened properly and want to do business with you, the best thing you can do is give the prospects what they want—a quick exit, not a couch and a psych exam.

➢ Earnest Money Deposits

You'll either be buying from FSBO houses or through Realtors®. If it's a FSBO, you'll use a purchase and sale agreement and put up a very small deposit, usually $10. In deals with motivated sellers, a deposit isn't an issue; sellers couldn't care less. You're only giving a deposit to show a monetary consideration.

Contrary to common belief, a deposit isn't even required. Consideration doesn't have to be in the form of money (it can be love and affection), but why risk a challenge? Just give up the $10 and get the seller to sign it's been received. My contract has a place at the end for sellers to sign confirmation of receiving a deposit. My cash flow systems contain all the documents you'll need. If you can't find them on your own, go to **www.RonLeGrand.com**.

Dealing with Realtors® is a wholly different ball game. All Realtors® use their contract, which is OK, and they'll want a much larger deposit—from a minimum of $1,000 depending on the size of the deal. But don't forget you're in control here. You decide how much you're willing to put up; if it's not reasonable, the Realtor® may not present your offer or you'll look foolish if the Realtor® does.

If you know you'll take the deal—you should if you use my MAO formula on junkers—and you have the deposit, you'll look like a professional with a decent deposit. However, the deal's at risk if you don't buy—that is, unless the seller can't deliver good title. So if you're gonna deal with Realtors®, you can expect to put up a deposit. I've put as much as $50,000 as earnest money. Of course, it was on a $5 million house, which may be scary to you but . . .

If you're going to run with the big dogs and pee in the tall grass . . . you got to get off the porch.

➢ Contingency Clauses

These are commonly referred to as "weasel" clauses—ways to get out if you change your mind. Most real estate courses tell you to load up your contract with them to protect yourself—but from what? The most you can lose is your deposit if you back out. No one can force you to buy. They don't put you in jail. They simply keep your deposit all of $10 if it's an FSBO.

Contingency clauses could fill up this book if I chose to write them. But, some good news for you is that weasel clauses are for people who aren't serious about buying property. The clauses are unprofessional, unnecessary, and cost you deals.

However, it means I'm using a Realtor® if my deposit is more than a few hundred dollars, and then I *will* protect myself. But, I only need one clause to do it in most cases; it's common and acceptable to institutional sellers who expect it. In fact, it's built into a lot of contracts on bank- owned property. When I made the offer on the $5 million house, I used a contingency clause and got my $50,000 deposit back when the value came in lower than represented by the Realtor®. Here's the clause:

This offer is subject-to a property inspection and appraisal suitable to and paid by buyer to be done within 30 days.

However, this will not work on bank owned deals. If you add any contingencies the deal is dead. The Realtor® likely won't present your offer and it's a waste of time if they do. No contingencies on bank deals.

That pretty much covers everything and anything you want it to and gives you time to verify your assumptions, including a home inspection, contractor estimate, and appraisal for the after repair value. If you don't buy after that, you *should* lose your deposit. It's only fair.

"If the offers aren't getting made, you aren't getting paid."

Ron LeGrand®

Ray Ritchie- Salisbury, NC

Ron,

It's been ten months since I attended your "Quick Start Real Estate," 4-day seminar. It was one of the first steps I used to re-invent myself to this current real estate market that had kicked me so hard in the stomach, so to speak. I knew the old ways of doing real estate I had used in the past had to change if I was to stay in real estate.

I love doing "Rent to Own" also known as "Lease to Own" and rehabbing properties. I was already thinking of ways to get the right marketing and forms system to use in this new market we're in. I saw the writing on the wall. Your ACTS program solved that problem for me.

Since that time, I have done 8 ACTS deals. I'm using a virtual assistant, and that system is working great for me.

Attached is a check for $13,250.00, which is the best deal I've done so far. I also received $1,000 from the tenant buyer to take the property off the market until closing, for a total of $14,250.00 after expenses!

Ron, I know you like to say I'm old as dirt, but I re-invented myself to this market with the best of the young studs!!

Thanks for your help!

Ray Ritchie

Chapter 10

Step 4 - Following Up

The most violated rule in business is the lack of follow-up. Most businesses are one-hit wonders whose owners quit immediately after a prospect says no.

Your job is to stay in the Loop with sellers *who pass the prescreening test* until they've sold the house or you've bought it. This applies to prospects now, not suspects. Get rid of the unmotivated sellers immediately and follow up with only the good prospects you can't quite come to terms with now. It'll pay handsome dividends. Remember: All sellers' minds will change with time and circumstance.

When a seller says no, it doesn't always mean no; it usually means please keep bugging me until the time is right for me to say yes. Here's an old marketing axiom that's true in all businesses, including real estate:

Eighty-two percent of all sales are made on the second through the seventh contact with a prospect.

When you give up too quickly you may be taking an 82 percent pay cut without even knowing it.

Have you ever said to yourself, *"This is the way it's going to be, by golly, and I'm not changing my mind?"* Then a while later you did a 180-degree reversal. Things happen, attitudes change. Sellers make payments on vacant houses, miss their loved ones who've already "moved on," are forced to leave town quickly, get into financial trouble, realize their house is not the only one available on the planet, get tired of "lookie loos," and are confronted with numerous other motivations for acting immediately. Hang in there until the time is right, and keep a communication link.

The next part of following up is to get a title check done immediately after getting a signed contract or deed. You can't lease or sell a property unless you know you can deliver good title to a buyer. All kinds of things can cloud title and create problems, some even unknown to the seller. Here are examples of some but definitely not all:

- An incorrect deed in the past chain of title
- Missing signatures
- Undisclosed marital status
- Forged checks
- Liens and judgments attached to the property
- Unfinished bankruptcy or even a current bankruptcy seller didn't disclose
- Un-notified creditors in past foreclosure proceedings
- Pending foreclosure

Heck, you don't even know for sure you're dealing with the right owner until you have a title search done. Have you heard about the fellow who waited until a couple of owners went on vacation and, while they were gone, had a fire sale of their homes at a dirt cheap price to five different buyers? All he did was take big earnest money deposits all weekend, sign contracts, and then skip town before the owners returned. Now he's getting free room and board, but he almost got away with it.

All you must do to have your title checked is call in a title search to a title company or to your attorney who'll want the address, the seller's name, and a legal description if you have it. A few days later you'll get a report if you request it and know if you have any problems. The cost for a title search ranges from $65 to $150, but many times you can get it done free if you develop a relationship with the title company and do constant business.

If a problem arises, you have four choices: (1) Ask the title company if it can fix the problem, (2) fix it yourself after the company tells you how, (3) make the seller handle it, or (4) back out of the deal. Any real estate contract will provide for the return of your deposit if there's a title problem.

If no problem exists, which is usually the case, you can move to step five, which is to sell quickly and is the subject of the next chapter.

"You may not get rich quick, but if you never get started, you'll never get rich."

Ron LeGrand®

Phil Van Buren- Southfield, MI

Here's the story:

I had clients that needed a place to move in while I was working on completing their short sale and this house was for lease on the MLS. The listing agent, however, never returned any of my calls so after a couple weeks I researched the owner and took a letter to his house indicating I had clients that wanted to lease but his agent was MIA. He called me back and said his agent was worthless and that I could take over the listing.

Meanwhile, my client's short sale fell through so they couldn't move around the same time I enrolled in Ron's Gold Club and somehow stumbled on to the ACTS concept. I didn't fully understand it but I knew there was more money there than what an agent would make leasing a house.

When I finally got the appointment to discuss paperwork with the owner, I took an ACTS lease with me and told him that a lease option was a far superior method than just leasing because of the pride of potential ownership. To my surprise, he did not even hesitate and signed the lease that night. I had to wait about 2 weeks for him to do some painting and cleaning and then I used craigslist and pointer signs to market the property. I think it only took three days to get a tenant buyer and maybe seven days total to close. I made about $5,000.

I'm currently training my VA and hope to get 2-3 leads per week before January is over. If I can get another deal discovered and closed before the end of January, I plan to come to Jacksonville for the Paper Power Boot Camp.

Ron you're a Genius!

Sincerely,

Phil Van Buren

Chapter 11

Step 5 - Selling Houses Fast

One of the most common fears people have about getting into real estate is the fear of being unable to sell a house and somehow getting stuck with it. I can understand why this fear would create anxiety for beginners because they simply don't have enough facts to overcome the fear. However, if you're not a beginner and the fear remains a problem, you have no excuse. So let's get it fixed right now.

The truth is that selling should be the easiest part of your business.

Are you not buying because you're waiting to sell what you have? Is your income suffering because you haven't plugged the hole in the back end? Are you so afraid of selling that you quit (or never started) buying?

In this chapter, I discuss the reasons why some people have trouble selling, how to dispose of the reasons, and a step-by-step process for selling wholesale deals, lease-options, and cash-out buyers. I've identified 14 reasons here why people have trouble selling houses. Pay close attention to reason numbers 4 through 7 because when combined, they amount to about 80 percent of the reasons that houses don't get sold quickly.

Most of the time it's a people problem, not a house problem.

These are the 14 main reasons why houses don't sell quickly:

1. *Not ready to sell*
2. *Poor area*
3. *Overpriced*
4. *Salesperson's personality problems*
5. *Inflexibility of seller*
6. *Salesperson's lack of knowledge about available financing programs*
7. *Salesperson's lack of knowledge about attracting and prescreening leads*
8. *No follow-up system in place*

9.   *Functional obsolescence*
10.   *House very small*
11.   *Salesperson losing control of loan process*
12.   *House too far from city*
13.   *House in price range too high for most buyers*
14.   *Only one bath*

Notice that the majority of these problems are directly related to the person in charge of making the sale; the rest should be fixed before you buy. Now let's examine some of these reasons for problems more carefully.

➤ *Not Ready To Sell*

- Front appearance: Would you want to see the inside?
- Roof: Does it need to be replaced?
- Exterior paint: Is it at least two colors and does it look fresh? Are the colors pleasing or gaudy?
- Interior paint: Is it two colors or does it look like a white tornado went through?
- Interior trim: Is there color, paper borders, blinds, bath and kitchen accessories, lever door handles, shower curtain or door, and so on?
- Carpet: Same old lifeless, ugly brown or have you tried hunter green?
- Would you want this carpet installed in your home?
- Central heat and air: If you're in the southern two-thirds of the country, it's not an option. Do it.
- Kitchen: Does it have plenty of cabinets or just enough to get by?

Customers won't complain about shoddy repairs. They just won't buy. If it doesn't look good enough to satisfy your wife, your buyers won't like it either. Spend a few more dollars and make it a house you can be proud to sell and one you know your buyer will rave to others about. If you do, amazing things will happen:

- It will sell quickly.

- It will appraise for more.
- You'll sleep better at night.
- Your buyers will send you customers.
- Your good reputation will spread quickly.
- The neighbors will send you customers or sell their houses to you.
- Your attitude will improve, and you'll enjoy dealing with buyers more because you know you have a great product.
- You'll save the extra money you spent in holding costs. So, in reality, all these benefits are free.

➢ Poor Area

- Is it a war zone? If so, you must learn to sell low-income houses, or else don't buy there if you intend to retail.
- In low-income areas it's critical you master the art of financing. You won't survive if all your sales must be to a qualified buyer or sold for 100 percent cash out. Get educated or get out of the war zones.

Here is the good news:

- You can make some large spreads on these houses because you can buy them dirt cheap.
- Most of your competition won't touch them.
- They're easy to find and easy to buy.
- At today's interest rates, buyers can qualify with small incomes.
- Financing is plentiful, some even with no down payment.
- You can always wholesale if rehabbing isn't feasible for you.

And the bad news:

- Vandalism is normal.
- You'll have to screen out a lot of buyers.
- You'll be tempted to break the law by falsifying down payments because most of your buyers are

broke. But, don't do it.

- ◆ You'll have to take back a lot of seconds, and 50 percent or more will default. So what? It's all free money anyway.

- ◆ If you're going to work the low-income or war zone areas, just be sure your exit is clear and you don't get into any traps. Don't rehab in a war zone unless you know where to get the buyer financed and you can live with vandalism.

In addition, you must be flexible on terms, not expect to get cashed out 100 percent, and clearly understand you will be prescreening one of the most uneducated segments of our society. It will take patience and practice.

➤ *Overpriced*

Overpriced is not what you think. Just for the record, all my houses are overpriced. And, I'm proud of it in case anyone asks. You should always set your sales price higher than the amount the house appraised for. If you don't ask for more, I can assure you that you won't get more.

But, there *is* a limit. Putting a $125,000 price on a $100,000 house is pushing the envelope, although putting a $109,900, or maybe even an $114,900 price on it may work fine.

Your market will tell you quickly. If all the buyers complain about the price, you know you have a problem and may want to lower the price a little.

Warning! Make sure the price is the problem before you start fixing what "ain't" broke. Only your buyers can tell you the price is too high—not your spouse, your neighbor, your brother-in-law, or especially your Realtor®. You can always lower the price, but you can't raise it once it leaves your lips. I don't know for sure, but I'd bet I haven't lowered the price on more than 15 percent of all the houses I've sold. As a rule, 10 percent above the appraised value or good comps is the upper limit. You'll have to decide the price based on the area, condition and salability of the house, and the heat of the market. Just don't give away money because you're listening to morons.

➢ Salesperson's Personality Problems

Have you ever talked to a seller or a Realtor® you didn't like—a mean-spirited, grouchy personality perhaps? How about someone who just won't shut up long enough for you to ask a question? Maybe you've encountered the pre-screener type who treats you like the enemy until you pass his or her qualification test.

How about all those times you got a wife on the phone, and she was afraid to speak without her husband's permission (or vice versa). That doesn't even count the ones who do talk but never say anything. Then there's the clueless spouse who can't even tell you the asking price, much less the other details. How about the couple in the middle of a divorce and the wife talks to you as though you're the one who just cheated on her?

Then there are the know-it-alls who want to do a seminar for you on the phone to impress you with their knowledge about the art of real estate. They can't sell their own house but can certainly tell you how to do it. Of course, we can't forget all the "thinker" brains trying to sell to the reptile brains and vice-versa. Or the sellers so in love with their house that it takes them 30 minutes to describe every little detail while you're trying to stay awake.

The key for you is to not become like one of those people I just described. If you already are, you can resolve the problem once it's identified. Here's a hot tip: Record your calls and listen to yourself selling your house. If there was a moron on the call, you'll probably recognize his or her voice. Every time you talk to a buyer, you must sound *friendly, flexible,* and *excited.* If you can't, then get someone else to sell your houses.

➢ Inflexibility Of Seller

This means that most sellers can see only one way to sell a home, and if that doesn't happen, the house will sit and sit until that perfect buyer comes along. Finding an A-credit buyer to cash you out isn't the only answer, especially true for low-income houses where A+ buyers are scarce.

The more you know about different exits, the easier it will be for you to become flexible. If you don't have your money in the deal and can live another week without the cash from the sale, you are freed up to get creative and look at other alternatives.

Here's a news flash for you: It's your job to find a buyer who loves your house... then make it work!

This means that sometimes you must be flexible. It's not a perfect world—bend a little. Here's a short list of selling methods:

- Sell to a qualified buyer and cash out now.
- Lease-option to your tenant-buyer and cash out later.
- Sell with owner financing and help the buyer get refinanced later.
- Sell with owner financing and sell the note at closing for 93 percent of its face value. We spend a whole day on this in the Paper Power class, which is part of our curriculum at Financial Freedom Academy.
- Get the buyer an 80 to 90 percent loan with a secondary lender at a higher rate and take back a second mortgage or deed of trust for the difference.

There's always another way.

➢ Salesperson's Lack of Knowledge about Available Financing Programs

If you're going to master your craft of selling houses, you must learn a lot about financing programs. What will kill loans? What programs require little or no down payment? What credit can be fixed and what can't? What will the lender want fixed before closing? Who will let you take back a second and who won't? And, add 40 or 50 other questions you'll get the answers to as you go. You don't have to know all there is to know about financing to sell a house, but the quicker you learn certain basics, the easier it gets. Make an appointment with three or four mortgage lenders and pick their brains. Let them help with what will work and what won't. Then when you get an interested prospect, it's simply a matter of getting the buyer's information to the lender of your choice and letting the lender tell you what will work.

That's the best way I know to learn the ropes about financing. But, a lot of veterans won't even take time to do this. I guess they feel they're too good or too smart to ask for help. My friend, what you knew about financing a year ago is not what you should know today. It changes monthly. You must stay on top to be the best. That will happen automatically if you're selling houses regularly, so don't worry about it.

➤ Salesperson's Lack of Knowledge about Attracting and Prescreening Leads

The first step to success in buying and selling is locating prospects; without potential buyers, it's very hard to sell houses. Frankly, an ad in the newspaper should be enough to attract plenty of prospects if you know how to write the ad and where to put it.

I can't turn this into an ad-writing course, but any ad that gets prospects to call is a good one. Any ad that doesn't is a bad one, or it's in the wrong publication. Make sure your ad gives the prospect a reason to call. Try to include a USP (unique selling proposition); what are you offering that everyone else isn't? For example:

Lease Purchase
No Qualifying Owner Financing
No Bank Qualification
No Money Needed
Easy Terms
Owner Will Help
Will Accept Anything on Trade
No Down Payment
You Get a Car with the House, and on and on

Some students use flyers distributed in newspapers and don't run ads. Others use a lot of signs, referrals, mail-outs, the

Internet, and electronic voice broadcasts.

The key is to make sure you keep a good flow of leads coming in until the house is sold. Where most people fail is in the way they handle leads once they come in. That, my friend, is by far the weakest link in the chain. Leads must be prescreened properly and the good ones worked daily. Out of any batch of leads will usually come some qualified ones—maybe not with A credit but qualified if you're flexible, as I discussed earlier what I look for most are people who love the house and are excited about owning it. Give me that and a little something to work with and I'll get them in it.

➤ No Follow-Up System In Place

The easiest way to sell houses is to work a buyers' list you built from the last house you sold. If you have more buyers than houses, you don't run ads, send flyers, mail letters, or any of that other stuff. You pick up the phone and call the prospects you've prescreened from the last time and tell them about your new house.

It's easier to suffer the pain of creating a buyer's list once rather than talking to dozens of prospects from ads every time you get ready to sell. You don't have to be an organizational wizard to do a little follow up. Hey, a pile of prescreened buyers on the corner of your desk with no separation or filing system is better than nothing. Sounds a little like my system, but at least I put them in a file folder. Then I misplace the folder, but I always know its close (somewhere).

➤ Functional Obsolescence

This one is a house problem, not a people problem. You usually can't fix it, so you shouldn't buy if it's present. That way you won't have trouble selling. Here are some things that come to mind:

- Extremely small rooms
- Bathroom off the kitchen
- Walk through bedroom to get to the only bath
- Low ceilings (under seven feet)

- House add-ons done unprofessionally
- Strange layout that can't be fixed
- House adjacent to odors, commercial property, school, or anything else that makes location undesirable
- Bad (or no) foundation

Those are just a few of the things I can think of now. Note: Sometimes you can correct them and sometimes you can't. If you don't see a way, simply pass.

➤ House Very Small

I guess this is also functional obsolescence, but it's very common. Any time a house has less than 1,000 square feet I get cautious. I've learned that houses under 1,000 square foot are usually hard to sell, and there's not much you can do but keep looking for a small family of one or two people. I'm not saying such houses won't sell. I'm just saying they're harder to sell. I've probably done 200 houses with areas of less than 1,000 square feet.

I think I own three or four now. I guess that verifies there is a buyer for every house. If I can buy such houses cheap enough, I'll still do so today. But, I know going in they may take a little longer to sell.

➤ Salesperson Losing Control Of Loan Process

You must remain in control from the moment you buy the house until you get a check. That includes the loan process. You decide who does the loan, who appraises the house, which gets the survey and termite report, and who closes. You are also in charge of speeding up the loan. Yep! You, not your lender.

You should check in every few days, push for results, and round up missing paperwork. If you don't, the close will drag on forever. Would you allow your boss to hold your paycheck for two to three weeks until she decides to pay you? That's exactly what you're doing when you let a loan processor jerk your chain. So the next time you lose a buyer because a loan processor didn't close quickly enough, go to your bathroom mirror and cuss out the person responsible.

The last time I lost a buyer two days before closing was because God told him not to buy. Had I been two days earlier, maybe I wouldn't have been competing with God. Oh well. Six weeks later I sold the house for $3,000 more than the first buyer. Maybe I wasn't competing with God after all.

➢ House Too Far From City

That's an easy one. Don't buy it unless you want to create a lot of driving time so you can listen to more of my CDs. Frankly, I don't buy anything I intend to retail that's more than 30 minutes from my office. Of course, I know for some in big cities that's about three blocks away. Hey, you can always move.

➢ House In Price Range Too High For Most Buyers

Sometimes the price has no bearing because the upper market is hot. If it is, the high value is not an excuse for a slow sale. The problem is elsewhere on this list. But in smaller cities, where a $500,000 house is a mansion, you can certainly expect selling to take much longer.

But that just makes a case for you to not guarantee monthly payments on big loans. Unless you're a sadist and looking for pain, you shouldn't try to outguess the market. Don't count on a high-priced house selling quickly just because you like it. Remove the risk, give yourself time, and you'll discover the big ones sell just like the little ones, but I hope with a lot more profit.

Caution. You'd better make sure you have a large spread on those big babies. Buyers of $500,000 homes are more sophisticated and more apt to ask for a price reduction. The good news is these folks can usually qualify for a loan, and the majority of the sales are all cash. Owner financing and lease purchase just don't have the sizzle they do on the lower end. That doesn't mean it's not used, only not as often.

➢ Only One Bath

I've sold hundreds of houses with only one bath, but it's

not my preference. Cheap houses—not a problem. Houses above $80,000 to $100,000, very difficult. And for houses much above $100,000, it's almost impossible. People who can pay more want more. If you can't add a bath, you may wish to consider not buying if you feel it's important to a sale.

I have never added a room on a house to add a bath. The only time I have added a bath, I've used the existing structure, which should cost you no more than $2,000 to $3,000. Trying to sell a four bedroom, one bath house ain't easy. Selling a three bedroom, one bath house is OK as long as the house is small. Selling a two bedroom, one bath house is the norm that buyers expect.

I won't guarantee that every problem you'll run into is on my list, but chances are that if you take a good look at this list the next time you're having trouble selling a house, I bet you'll find the problem on it. If you do run into something out of the ordinary that I've not discussed here, drop me a line. In the meantime, remember there are no real problems, just solutions. And very often when you do run across a problem property, there's hidden profit there for someone who knows the answers and can create a solution.

➤ A Step-By-Step Process For Selling

Here you are with your first deal under contract to buy, lease-option, or option and only a few days or weeks from cashing in. That's great, but before we start the process of selling junkers to a bargain hunter or lease-optioning a house to a family or finding a qualified cash buyer, we must complete a very important step.

Either a title company or an attorney must do a title search to verify no liens are on the property other than those disclosed by the seller. The title company or attorney will also verify that the current owner is the only owner and there are no other parties of interest. Until this process is complete, you're not ready to sell or lease the house. Most states allow title companies to close real estate transactions, although some require attorneys to close. A call to a local title company will provide the answer.

Ugly Houses to Wholesale

If the property you're buying is an ugly house that was listed with an agent, the agent will want to handle this for you. Simply ask who he or she intends to call for the title work and say you'd like to handle the title yourself. If no agent is involved, you'll need to call a title company from the phone book, from a referral, or from a real estate agent. You'll need the legal description of the property to order a title search. If the house is listed, your real estate agent will provide it. If not, you can get the legal description from the seller's deed of mortgage or from public records with your database service.

If you're wholesaling a junker, either call or visit the title company or attorney or choose another company or attorney. Hold a short conversation with the one you choose about an assignment of contract, making sure your closing agent won't be a problem when it comes time to close. This is important to ensure the continuity of your deal. Agree on a price for this service (closing) before you order a search. The cost should not exceed $100; if it does, shop around.

If you're checking the title on a pretty house you intend to lease-option to a tenant-buyer, yon should make it clear you won't be closing right away but will be leasing the house. In such a case, you won't need a title policy at this time, only a search. Therefore, the fee you negotiate will come out of your pocket and be a cost of doing business.

Don't let your Realtor® get wind you are doing an assignment of contract. Make certain your title agent doesn't divulge this information either. When you're satisfied the closing agent will perform without becoming an obstacle, you may order a title check and deliver a copy of your purchase agreement and assignment of contract if you're doing a closing on a wholesale deal. In the case of a lease-option, your title agent won't need an agreement because you're not closing at this time.

If you don't feel comfortable with your conversation with the closing agent, find another agent. This whole process should take place within three days after you get an agreement to buy, lease, or option in your possession.

Step 1. *Getting Ready to Sell*

Once you know the title is clear, the next move is to prepare the house for sale. This won't be difficult because in most cases you're selling it in its "as is" condition as an ugly house. If it's a pretty house deal, the house should be in good condition so the only concern is when it can be occupied. When wholesaling a house, you won't need to put up a For Sale sign, and in fact, you shouldn't put one up in most cases as you don't own the house.

A sign isn't necessary and may attract attention from the seller or agent if placed without permission. If you're using an agent and buying an institutionally owned house, you'll find it difficult to get possession of the property during escrow or permission to clean it up and get a key. It becomes a liability issue.

If the seller is not an institution, it's much easier. You can do pretty much what you can get permission to do. If the yard needs cleaning or the house is trashed and you don't mind getting it cleaned up, simply ask. You should be able to get a key as well. However, you are not to spend much money or make any alterations to a house you don't own. Remember, you are selling "as is" for a wholesale price; your buyer is getting a good deal because of the condition of the house. The most you'll do is clean up the premises and secure the doors and windows—usually you won't even do that.

If you're doing a lease-option, there shouldn't be anything for you to do to the house except wait until it's vacant and ready to rent. When the house is vacated or about to be, it's time to start attracting tenant- buyers. If you're forced to do some minor cleaning up or carpet shampooing, make sure this gets done before showing the house. Again, this should involve a little work at most—not an expenditure of more than $100 or $200. Once you have possession, place a Lease/Purchase or For Sale by Owner sign in the front yard. You can have it made at any sign shop, or you might find a sign in a supply store; you can also go to **www.RonLeGrand.com/Resources**.

Step 2. *Attracting Buyers*

It's now time to run an ad whether you're wholesaling, leasing, or cashing out. I'll start with the wholesaling process. Run an ad in the daily paper under "Investment Properties" or a similar column; a three-day ad should be sufficient and should read:

Handyman special, cheap, cash
[Your phone number]

Of course you'll want to put all over the sites in your area, especially those you get free. See the resources section.

Don't add anything to the ad. If the paper insists you put in anything else, fight hard to not allow it, although changing the word *handyman* to *handyperson* is acceptable if the paper insists. Make sure you or someone working with you is available to take or return calls.

Don't volunteer information. Answer only what you're asked and send the prospects to the house you have advertised. Tell them to get in if they can and just look if they can't. When asked what you want for the house, be prepared with your answer and don't sound wishy-washy. If you've used my formula for making an offer and are reasonably close on your ARV and repairs, your asking price should be at or about the MAO, which should be at least $5,000 more than you agreed to pay.

Be sure to build a buyers' list in the process. It will become your most important asset as a wholesaler. Keep track of the number of calls and emails you receive. You are not to visit the house with your callers. They'll call you back if they're interested; if they don't, you call them. If a prospect who wants to buy hasn't contacted you within five days after your placing the ad, extend the ad for five days. Continue this process until you get a buyer who wants to meet and give you a $500 deposit.

If you're dealing with a tenant-buyer for a pretty house, you want to run an ad in your daily paper in the area that matches the location of the house. Make sure the words *lease* and *purchase* are in the ad.

Running an ad for ten days at a time is sufficient in the paper, but you should keep it on the local sites. You can always cancel or extend as needed. Don't put the required deposit or monthly rent requested in the ad. As the calls come in, be sure to capture information from the prospects who sound interested. Send the prospects to see the house. Make certain they can look into all the windows, but you are not to show the house until the prospect calls you back and expresses an interest. Let the house show itself. In fact, most of my successful students, as well as myself, buy a lockbox from Home Depot to install on the front door with a key inside it. Now, instead of meeting prospects at the house, you can give them the lockbox code and let them look on their own. If they like what they see, you'll get a call if you leave flyers on the counter with all the facts about the house and your phone number.

I know this sounds scary at first, but you'll quickly discover the risk of buyers' stealing something (from a vacant house) is far easier to deal with than making numerous trips to show houses to people who frequently don't show up.

"The Less I Do, the More I Make."

Never tell the callers what you want for a deposit. Always ask what they have to work with first. Those with the most cash will rise to the top of your list. Those with little or no money should be quickly discarded unless they have good credit, in which case they become buyers you get financed now with the numerous no-money-down, first-time home buyers' programs available.

Step 3. *Prescreening Buyers*

Again, let's start by prescreening calls on houses you wish to wholesale to bargain hunters. You've run a handyman special ad and getting calls from prospective buyers. You've sent several to the property and now one who shows serious interest calls you back and says he or she wants the house.

Ask your buyer when he or she would like to close. If the

answer is ASAP, you have a real prospect. Any other answer is not acceptable unless you're convinced your buyer is real and can perform. If the buyer needs to see the inside and couldn't gain entry on his or her own, you'll have to make arrangements for getting in. If no agent is involved, this can be done easily by getting a key from the owner if you haven't already done so.

If an agent is involved, ask the agent if you can get a key to show the house to prospective contractors. Most will cooperate, but some won't. If this presents a problem, you may be forced to have an agent meet you at the property with the buyer or tell the buyer you don't have a key and can't get in at this time.

You'll be surprised to learn that when you leave enough profit on the table for your buyer, the buyer will usually find a way in or agree to buy without entry. Your common sense applied to the circumstances surrounding the deal will guide you to the right choice here. Use your own judgment.

You never need to meet your buyer. Ask the buyer to send a check made out to you for $500. Have the assignment of contract prepared and ready to sign. If you have set a fair sales price, don't come off that price; just tell your buyer that's the least you can accept. Show no flexibility. Once you have a signed contract to sell along with a deposit, you may move to the next step.

Now let's move to prescreening tenant-buyers for lease-purchase or cash-out deals. When prospects who have inspected the house call back to see the inside, prescreen them before setting an appointment. If they have no money, have no credit, or can't afford the monthly payment, you don't need to meet them. Make an appointment only if you feel good about the chances of the prospects' buying. Good credit may or may not be necessary; this will depend on the situation. However, a substantial earnest money deposit is always necessary for you to install a lease-option tenant. No exceptions!

Meet prospects at the house or let them go through the house by themselves and leave some sample applications on the counter. The application must state they're granting you permission to check their credit. Tell them you'll let them know within two days and secure their deposit. The bigger the deposit, the better. Get at least $500 at this point and more if you can.

Make the prospects aware that this deposit is refundable if you can't accept them. Let them know when they can expect to meet your mortgage broker to complete the paperwork. If they're approved your mortgage originator can obtain the remainder of the deposit and run a credit report and tell you what kind of loan he/she can get your prospect.

If your intent is to lease-option, you simply need to know what you're dealing with. Credit won't be your main criterion for selecting a tenant-buyer, but you should always know with whom you're dealing before accepting a prospect.

If you're looking for a qualified buyer to cash you out now, it's simply a matter of letting your mortgage broker or loan processor guide you on what kind of loan is available for your buyer. If you like what you hear, pass it on to your buyer and let the processor take it from there, arranging a meeting to get an application. You bow out and let the processor get a loan completed.

If you don't like what you hear, simply return the deposit and move on.

More Magic Words When Selling

Now let's look at the selling side and discuss a few choice words I use to find good buyers. When wholesaling, I want to know my buyer will come to closing with the money and isn't simply trying to jerk my chain. In this case, the magic words are "When do you want to close?" If the buyer needs more than ten days, he or she is a time waster and I'm at risk. If the buyer says "ASAP," I know the buyer's serious.

So many magic words are available when prescreening prospective buyers for pretty houses that it's easier to simply use the whole script—all these words are magic. I can't tell you how many hundreds, maybe thousands, of buyers I talked to before I developed the words and the order in which I use them. Here we go:

"Do you want to buy or rent?"

If the answer is rent and you want to sell, the rest is worthless conversation. But before giving up, use one more line: *"Have you ever tried to buy before?" "Yes." "What stopped you?"*

This lets you know immediately what you're dealing with.

"Is your credit good, fair, or ugly?"

Don't ask, "How's your credit?" Some people are ashamed to tell you it's ugly and will simply lie. Give them a multiple- choice question so they know you won't be shocked if they have poor credit. If it's bad:

"What's on it a bank wouldn't like?"

This breaks the ice and gets the customer to open up. Now the big question:

"How much money can you raise for a down payment?"

Whatever the answer:

"Can you get any more?"
"Can you borrow more from relatives?"
"Do you have credit cards?"
"Do you have something you could sell or trade to me?"
"Can you repair houses or have other skills to earn more?"

Now let's assume you see someone you can work with and you want that prospect to get excited and realize that you are his or her solution to home ownership. Here are the words that will glue that person to you:

"If you can convince me you want the house and make a commitment to buy, I'll get you financed one way or another. Even if I have to be the bank. If I can't get you in a home of your own, no one in this city can."

These words have sold a lot of real estate for me. They really make an impact on your buyer's level of hope. Follow them up with assurance that you are easy to work with and very flexible and the prospect will be putty in your hands:

> *"We can do whatever you and I agree. I own the house and I'll do what takes if you will. Is that fair?"*

Well, that ought to be enough magic to keep you practicing a while. Of course, these words aren't really magical until you begin to actually use them and make them work.

Step 4. *Closing the Sale*

If you're wholesaling a junker, deliver both contracts to your closing agent by fax or in person to set up a closing. If a Realtor® is involved, you must notify him or her of the time and place, but remember that you should be in control of the process. Simply call the agent and coordinate a time suitable to your buyer and the seller.

Call the buyer with the time and place as well as the closing agent's telephone number. A cashier's check is normally required to close, so the buyer will need a little time to acquire it. If the seller isn't present, it means the closing package has been completed by mail prior to your closing.

Attend the closing. While there, your job is to sit back, be quiet, and let your closer do his or her job. You'll be surprised how quickly it will happen. Once the buyer has come and gone, all that's left for you to do is get a copy of the file and your check. Make a copy of your check and submit it to me with a short letter discussing your success.

Now let's move on to our lease-option buyer. If you like your prospect set an appointment to meet. Go over the terms of the agreement and meet on all issues, including the length of the lease, the late penalty, repairs, pets, the purchase price, the option deposit, and the monthly rent. While you're together, call your attorney and set an appointment for your buyer to sign a lease and an option agreement. *Do not prepare these documents yourself Let your attorney handle it.*

Make certain tenant-buyers know they need to bring with them the balance of the deposit money as well as the first month's rent and the attorney's fee.

It's important you don't practice law here. There are several reasons why I strongly suggest you let your attorney handle the signing party:

- The attorney will prepare the agreements so you don't have to.
- It's free for you; your buyer will pay the $200 to $300 cost.
- Your buyer will know the agreements are professionally done and will feel more comfortable with the deal after the excitement wears off.
- There is less chance of the buyer demanding the return of the option deposit later when he or she decides to move. This is non-refundable money, as your attorney (and the agreement) will clearly spell out and receive acknowledgment.
- If you ever do get into a dispute, there's no better witness than the attorney who closed the lease, explained the rules, and prepared the documents.

If you want an excellent lease-option agreement, whether the houses are pretty or you're installing a work-for-equity tenant, you can go to **www.RonsGoldClub.com** and join. It has dozens of forms and agreements. The lease- option agreements I spent $6,000 to have prepared are on the site along with a list of benefits as long as your arm.

OK! The only kind of buyer left is one who's applying for a loan and closing the deal before moving in. The old-fashioned way: cash out now.

At this point you've already talked to your loan processor and determined if your prospect will get a loan for an amount you can live with. If it's a go, simply have the processor call the prospect to take the long form application and check in from time to time on the progress. When all the documents are in, you go to the closing and pick up a big check. The last step is to take your family out to the finest restaurant in town and celebrate. Don't forget to tell them why and to make an announcement every time you close a deal you're celebrating. Watch how fast they get interested in your business. A few trips to fun places would also help to increase the excitement level.

Here are the steps in a line-by-line format with some additions I didn't mention above:

Wholesaling a Junker

1. *Get a contract to buy.*
2. *Check the title.*
3. *Run an ad.*
4. *Send callers to the house.*
5. *Get an assignment of contract and a deposit from the buyer.*
6. *Send the assignment of contract to the closing agent with an agreement to buy after you have a clarifying conversation. Have the agent notify the buyer and the seller.*
7. *Attend the closing and pick up the check.*
8. *Celebrate and do it again.*

Selling to a Tenant-Buyer

1. *Get the deed or lease-option agreement from the seller.*
2. *Check the title.*
3. *Get ready to sell if the house needs work.*
4. *Run ads and place signs.*
5. *Send callers to the house with lock box code. Leave info on the counter.*
6. *Get credit application over the phone or in person and send to the mortgage broker or loan processor if either has at least a 3 percent deposit.*
7. *Determine your next move based on the report from processor. If it's a go, move to the next step.*
8. *Set up a meeting and get the money.*
9. *Set up an appointment with your attorney.*
10. *Send attorney the facts to fill out the lease and option.*
11. *Let attorney close and send you the lease agreement and remaining funds from the deposit and/or first month's rent.*
12. *Celebrate and do it again.*

Selling Houses to Buyers with New Financing Now—Cash Out

1. *Get a deed, lease-option, or option signed by the seller or purchase all cash with a private lender.*
2. *Check the title.*
3. *Renovate the house and get it ready to sell.*
4. *Run ads and place signs.*
5. *Send callers to the house with lock box code. Leave info on the counter.*
6. *Get the credit application on the phone or in person if prospect states his or her credit is good or fair.*
7. *Determine your next move based on the report from processor. If a loan is available, you can accept move to the next step.*

    a. *Let processor set up a meeting to get application and deposit if you haven't done so already.*
    b. *Check in from time to time.*
    c. *Go to the closing and pick up check.*
    d. *Celebrate.*

I know this doesn't cover everything you'll ever need to know to sell houses. In *fact*, I could write a book on any process I just described that we do in a four-day training event called Quick Start Real Estate School, **www.RonsQuickStart.com.** Then there's the auction method, the round-robin method, staging houses, how to sell high-dollar houses, problem houses, getting weak borrowers qualified, autopilot systems to build a huge buyers list using technology, marketing tools, and numerous other subjects to fill an entire book.

I know I sound like a broken record but if all this stuff interests you, do yourself and your family a favor and get some quality training from the pros who walk the walk. Go to **www.RonsQuickStart.com** or call **800-567-6128** and ask about our training.

"Most people give up just when they're about to achieve success. They quit on the one-yard line. They give up at the last minute of the game, one foot from a winning touchdown."

Ross Perot

Kyle & Camille Davis- Houston, TX

Mentors,

Is this for real? This is no longer a question of ours! Mentors are FOR REAL! Here is yet another deal we have done while under their wings. Take a look –

We took over this property Subject To with only $74,412 remaining balance. ARV is $135,000. We bought the property for $25,000 leaving remaining equity of approx. $35,000. We used a private lender to fund the $25k paying $200 per month.

We just leased the property with an option to purchase in 3 years. They will owner finance it from us for $135,000 with $25,000 down payment and 10% interest for 22 years. We received $2,275 up front to be used toward down payment. There are some minor repairs needed which the leasers agreed to take care of themselves to include electrical and updating bathrooms, otherwise we would have listed it around $145k owner finance.

Monthly payments to the bank are $725.09 (PITI) and $200 monthly payment to private lender. Monthly rent payment coming in at $1400....A $474.91 per month cash flow while leasing. This will increase some more when our own insurance kicks in.

When owner finance - $135,000 purchase price minus $22,725 down payment = $112,275 financed amount. Will pay off the private lender with down payment and begin to receive $328.33 monthly cash flow for the next 22 years with no money out of our pocket. Total profit over the 25 year period is $17,096.76 rent profit over the first 3 years and then another $86,679.12 for the remaining 22 years for a grand total of **$103,775.88**. This will help toward retirement.

This deal included the following methods:
- Subject To
- Lease with Option to Purchase
- Work for Equity
- Owner Finance (wrap around mortgage)

Kyle & Camille Davis

Chapter 12
Where To Get The Money With No Credit Or Partners

Back in the early 1980s, I got this notion that I wanted to be a real estate investor. I had seen an ad that read "Come learn to buy real estate with no money down." The thought appealed to me, especially as I was struggling to make a living, and the one thing I didn't have was cash or credit. My whole focus, from morning to night, was how to get enough money coming in so I could keep my old beat-up jalopy running and pay my bills. I worked long hours, doing everything I could to stay ahead of the rat race because I was brought up to believe that all it takes to get rich is working hard and keeping your nose clean. Boy, wasn't that a load of baloney?

I wasn't concerned then that my family and I could lose everything because, frankly, we didn't have a whole lot to lose. We had already filed for bankruptcy a few years earlier, which was devastating to my confidence and my ego. All the assets we owned were stuffed into a 1,000 square-foot house that my dad had helped me buy by loaning me the money to assume a VA loan. The one thing I hadn't lost, and by far the most important, was my burning desire to get more out of this life than a job and mere survival. I knew there had to be more out there than making a living. I just didn't know what it was. I can remember times when my will to win in these circumstances caused me so much anxiety that I hated to get out of bed in the morning. Each day was just as boring and uneventful as the last, and I didn't have any answers to how to change things, let alone improve them.

I was broke and bankrupt, felt worthless, and was headed nowhere. How could a guy like me ever expect to make any real money? I had nothing to work with. At least, that's what I thought at the time, but that burning desire just wouldn't rest until I found a way . . . and that's what compelled me to attend my first real estate seminar, even though I had to borrow the money to go. The difference between me and many others is that burning desire. Without it, you don't stand a chance of making any real money. You see, the same desire that compelled me to attend that seminar also compelled me to use what I learned there and to stick with it. It would have been so much easier to quit when the first obstacle arose.

But I didn't quit, and the rest is history. I believe the main reason I can communicate so well with beginning investor's lies within my humble beginnings. In a nutshell, *I've never forgotten the gut-wrenching anxiety that comes with being broke, and I never will!* Now you may he asking yourself what all this has to do with raising money to do deals, just bear with me, and you'll see my reason for telling you this tear-jerking story. In fact, there are three:

1. I want you to get a feel for where I was when I began as an entrepreneur so that the next time a stupid thought such as "You gotta have money to make money" enters your head, you'll think of me and immediately come to your senses.
2. I want you to understand that no success comes without sleepless nights and plenty of anxiety.
3. When you start using what I'm about to teach you, you'll experience rejection, which may bring some anxiety. With time and success, that anxiety will go away— especially if you persist until you win. If you quit, however, the anxiety of being a loser never goes away.

➢ Where To Get The Money

Not knowing where to get the money to do deals keeps a lot of people out of the business and, unfortunately, costs them financial freedom. And, that saddens me because it's the easiest hurdle to overcome. Before we talk about where to get the money, let's discuss what we could do with it if we had it. I wouldn't use it to buy pretty houses—you simply don't buy attractive houses in nice neighborhoods priced at retail value and pay cash for them. And, you won't get them at wholesale price because there is no reason for the seller to discount.

Because the only time I'd pay cash for a house is when I buy at wholesale price, cash isn't necessary to deal in houses needing no repairs. For those houses I use lease-options, options, owner financing, or debt takeover, all of which require little or no cash when done properly. When we're in the wholesaling business, our job is to find houses that can be bought at wholesale price and quickly flip them to retailers.

We find the bargains and pass them on to the bargain hunters quickly. This doesn't require cash because the buyer brings the money to purchase from you. Then the closing agent subtracts what you agreed to pay and cuts you a check for the difference. The only cash you need is for an earnest money deposit. That's almost never more than a few hundred dollars and usually less than $100 when dealing with sellers directly.

So, we don't need to raise money to do 90 percent of the business. The money comes from our buyer at a simultaneous closing or we simply don't need it to do the deal if we're properly trained. That leaves only one type of deal that does require money: buying a house and rehabbing it. This requires money but certainly not yours. So let's discuss how I solved the money problem when I began.

My first seminar taught me a few techniques about how to find deals, so the first thing I did was start looking. I found a Realtor® to help me find junkers from the MLS book, and it wasn't long before my offer on a small fixer-upper was accepted.

I remember my Realtor® asking me several times if I had the money. I simply gave her the answer I had learned in class: "The money's on the way." Now I didn't have a clue where it was coming from, but I knew if I could find a good deal, I shouldn't have too much trouble finding a money partner. As it turned out, I was right.

I took the deal to my ex-boss and he liked it. He put up some of the money and went to the bank to borrow the rest. That was the beginning of a partnership that lasted six months and 23 deals until I found a source of funds that eliminated my having to share 50 percent of every deal. This source supplied all the money I needed to buy junkers as long as I bought them cheaply enough—which launched me into a whole new career. My new source was a mortgage broker, whom I promised I'd make famous; his name is Al Coplan, hereafter referred to as Al.

Al's job as a one-man brokerage company was to pair private lenders, who had money to invest, with borrowers like me, who could bring him safe loans. Al didn't care about my credit or my income. His only concern was the collateral for the loan. When he put out money for his friends, relatives, and other private lenders, he had a simple system: If the loan went bad, he was responsible for doing whatever it took to make sure the lender didn't lose money, even if that meant coming out-of-pocket. Throughout our relationship, Al was adamant about his loan requirements. Put simply, his entire system revolved around one basic rule: *If I can't take the property back for the loan amount plus costs and make money, I won't do the loan.*

You see, Al didn't care about credit or income because it was, and still is, totally irrelevant to the safety of the loan. The only real insurance then was, and still is now, a low loan-to-value ratio. He simply wouldn't make a loan for more than 50 percent of the value of the property based on his appraiser's report. Of course, the downside was that these loans were high priced. The rate was 18 percent and Al got ten points off every loan (that's an extra 10 percent just for his services!). If that wasn't bad enough, his lenders got six additional months of interest every time I paid a loan off early, as I always did. Yes, the price was high, but it didn't take me long to figure out it was still cheaper than 50 percent to a partner plus I kept total control.

The upside was that Al would loan on the after-repair value, not the purchase price. This was critically important to an investor who was buying houses for 20 to 40 percent of their value because the houses needed work. He would escrow for repairs, but I became good at buying houses cheap enough for his loans to cover all the costs and the repairs, even when he withheld money until the work was finished. This meant that in every case I was borrowing much more than the purchase price.

We would close the loans a few days after the appraisal came back. No credit reports, no income verifications, and no other qualifying obstacles. Al provided a readily available source of funds for anyone who could live with a loan no higher than 50 to 60 percent of the appraised value. The cost was high, but as I quickly learned:

The cost of the money is irrelevant. It's the availability that's important.

As a borrower, my association with Al lasted several years. He made a lot of money for me and vice versa. Al is in business to this day and hasn't changed a thing so far as I know. In fact, I'm gonna send him this book when it's finished so he'll know I kept my promise to make him famous!

It took me a few years to figure out that if I could find my own private lenders, I wouldn't have to pay Al 10 percent of every loan to find them for me. It also occurred to me that I too could lend money and collect those 10 percent checks. All I had to do was get a mortgage broker's license, which is exactly what I did.

By using money from my own private lenders for deals, I don't pay a brokerage fee. A basic fact of business: When you go directly to the source, you don't have to pay a middleman (broker). Just in case you haven't figured it out by now, here's my point:

The best source of money you'll ever find for deals is from people just like you who'd like a higher rate of return than what they get from the bank. There are more private lenders fitting that description than you'll ever need.

They're easy to find, once you learn how, and it's an inexhaustible supply of money. You don't need credit or committees, and you can have the money a few days after finding the deals. You'll be a hero to your lenders because they will be receiving a very high rate of return safely. So let's spend some time learning first how to find these folks and then how to convince them to loan you their money.

As I said earlier, they are all around you. They're people just like you and from all walks of life. You're not looking for huge pools of money from pension plans, banks, or insurance companies. Focus on small amounts of money from everyday folks that will be money in their IRAs or money they have in stocks, bonds, CDs, savings accounts, or other investments. I've found IRAs a very easy source to tap for two reasons: First, making loans is an approved use of a self-directed IRA if it's with the right company as discussed later in the book; second, it's money most people consider off limits until retirement, so it's been sitting there doing nothing but getting low return.

Once you show prospects how much faster their money grows at 7-10 percent as opposed to 1 percent from a bank and point out its all tax deferred, it's simply not a hard sell. Yes, 7 percent is the rate I offer all my lenders.

So the first hurdle you have to overcome is to get your greed glands in check. If you go cheapskate and try to lower the rate, you'll get a lot less cooperation. Just remember that people who invest money do so for one reason only: to *make* money. If you take away the financial gain, you take away the incentive. Better to pay too much than too little. Better to have happy lenders who can't wait to tell their friends than wishy-washy lenders who have to be begged. If you make it worth their while and come through on what you promise, they'll soon be begging you to get rid of their money.

On the other hand, don't spoil them. Offering 18 percent only creates a question of high risk and costs you more money. A 7 to 10 percent return is enough to create excitement, and sometimes you can do better than that with people who know you and trust you. The best way to set a rate is to simply ask a few potential lenders what it will take to get them interested. If they are happy with 5 percent, don't kill the goose.

In order to borrow someone's IRA; it must be set up with a TPA (third-party administrator) who can fund the loan. Most IRAs aren't set up this way. It's no big deal to transfer, but you must help lenders take this preliminary step. Here's how: Go to **www.RonLeGrand.com/Resources** and ask for several IRA transfer packages. Once you have them, you can hand one to your new lender when the need arises. Your lender simply fills in the form, and mails it or they can go online and do the same. The TPA does the rest.

It takes about ten days to do the transfer. When it's completed, your lender simply faxes a request for the money to the closing agent, and the TPA will promptly reply by wiring money if requested. So, you're ready to close as soon as the money arrives.

If an IRA is not involved, you're ready to close as soon as you convince your private lender and get the title checked. One of the great advantages of private borrowing is fast closings. I close almost all my loans the day after I get the funds to the closing agent, which is always the day after my lender commits. We're talking five to seven days after the ink dries on the purchase contract if the seller is ready, and that includes appraisal time.

The question I ask prospective lenders is simple, to the point, and prequalifies them quickly: "Do you have an IRA or other investment capital that's not getting you a 12 percent return safely?" If they answer yes, they're either lying or not a prospective lender. If they answer no, the next thing you must do is find out if they even have an IRA or other money. The easiest way I've found to do this is follow up my first question with "Would you like to?" They'll either say yes or "I'd love to, but I don't have an IRA or other investments." This is where you either explain the program or go on to a qualified prospect.

You won't have to ask too many people before you get positive results if the following three conditions are met:

1. Your prospective lender must be qualified.
2. You must have some semblance of credibility.
3. You must be able to prove your case, not just expect your prospect to accept your word.

We've already discussed how to quickly prequalify your prospective lender with a couple of questions. So what do I mean by a semblance of credibility? I mean that you must look and act like someone who can be trusted and is competent to deal with another person's money. Do you dress professionally? Are your shoes shined and your hair neatly cut? If you feel you lack credibility, ask yourself (or someone who knows you and will be honest) why, and remedy it. More often than not, correcting the problem is as easy as getting a haircut and buying a nice shirt and a new pair of shoes.

If you feel you lack credibility from lack of experience, don't sweat it. Proving your case and acting with enthusiasm will overcome a lack of experience. If you think your young age presents a credibility problem, the same holds true. Act with enthusiasm and confidence and you'll get results.

Your biggest selling tool is the fact that you can protect your lender so well with equity. Point out that in a worst-case scenario the property will pay even if you can't. Talk about high return, safety, and how you want a lasting relationship with people who can mutually profit from your sweat.

Show your prospective lenders exactly what your intentions are for the property. Don't ignore the negatives and don't glorify the positives. Tell it like it is, tell the lenders how they win, convince them you're looking out for their investment and show them how all the proper paperwork will be done. Put them in touch with your closing agent or attorney and answer all their questions truthfully. By going through all these steps like a pro, you'll instill confidence in your prospective lenders and infect them with your enthusiasm. You simply won't have to beg anyone to lend you money. It's just not hard to convince people that 7 percent is better than the ½ or 1 percent that they're probably getting now.

You Won't Have to Beg

As a beginner, you'll have to prove your ability. But once you have a track record and a good reputation, that won't be necessary. Your word and a mortgage or trust deed will be all you'll need.

But for now, let's look at what a lender would like to see to feel at ease with the deal and you. Actually, this package is no different from the one you should compile before you buy a house. Your lender will probably want to see an appraisal and possibly a repair estimate before committing to the loan and may even want to see the house. If so, a complete repair estimate is very important to convince a lender that the cost is near the amount you think it is.

Furnish lenders a list of the closing documents they will receive. Or better yet, have them call your attorney or title company. By proving the value of the house with an appraisal and providing the proper documents after closing, you'll have shown professionalism and built a case for safety. These items should be included in a lender's package:

- Appraisal of the after-repair value
- Title insurance furnished by the closing agent
- Fire insurance naming the lender as mortgagee
- Original note prepared by the closing agent
- A copy of the mortgage or deed of trust—the closing agent will record the original and forward it to your lender
- A list of repairs and possibly an estimate of costs

Remember, the first step is to get moving and start asking. You may have to *"kiss some frogs,"* but that's the price of success. You'll be surprised at how few people you have to ask to get good results.

Just keep in mind how easy your job of buying houses will become once you can stop worrying about where the money will come from. At least 400 of the 3,000 houses I've bought have been financed with private loans through the method I've just shared with you.

I can't tell you how much that means in profit, but I know it beats the heck out of any job I've ever had! I'm sure you'll feel the same way once you do what it takes to get the money flowing. It will get easier each time you ask. Before long, you'll have more funds available than you can use all by yourself. That's when it's time to start making money as a mortgage broker yourself, just like my friend Al and me.

➢ It Takes Money To Make Money And Other Big Lies

Those who've said it takes money to make money were people trying to justify why they're broke. It doesn't take money to make money—at least not your money and frequently none at all. The truth is that if you can't make money without money, you can't make money *with* money!

When I started in 1982, I had no money or credit as I noted earlier. I was broke. I had no credit cards, no rich relatives, not even a wife working to support me. I'd quit my job and burned the ships behind me. The only way out was to make it or get another job. I had a mortgage and bills just like everyone else, yet somehow I made it happen. I succeeded in spite of the odds stacked against me.

You wanna know why? I succeeded *because* I had no money or credit! Believe it or not, *having* money and credit when you begin your career as a real estate entrepreneur can do you more harm than good. It can ruin you if you're not careful. Having no money keeps you focused on doing the deals that don't require money. If your credit sucks, as mine did, you can't apply for bank loans. Therefore, you inadvertently avoided the two biggest mine fields—not because you were so smart but because you had no choice. Whether you have money or not, you should learn to leverage your brain, not your wallet. When you do that, having money becomes a non-issue because you don't need it to buy houses. If you write big checks, you're always worried about losing those checks. If you guarantee loans, you risk everything you own. Do neither, and you eliminate your risk. I've said those words a thousand times, and I still see people who should know better doing it anyway.

Don't get me wrong; I'm not saying you shouldn't have money. I'd actually prefer you to be filthy stinking rich! I'm just saying you'll get there a lot quicker if buying houses doesn't depend on your capital or the number of loans you can borrow. Because if it does, you're a slave to your limited resources, and your business will move at a snail's pace.

How many loans can you get before you get cut off? Only a handful! Then what? How many deals can you buy if you have to write a check for each? You get the drift. On the other hand, how many loans can you take "subject-to" before you get cut off? That's right, there is no limit! And, no one's counting because it's endless. You can buy 500 houses and never ask permission or fill out an application to submit to a brainless loan officer.

The loans are not on your credit, and you aren't personally liable. If disaster, such as a deep recession, strikes before the loans are paid off, it's now the bank's problem, not yours. ("Subject-to" means the loan stays in the seller's name, but title transfers to you.) You can learn more about this from the TERMS course and the Quick Start Real Estate School. **www.RonsPrettyHouseSystem.com; www.RonsQuickStart.com**

If you're buying junkers to rehab, how many private loans can you get before you're cut off? All you want! You should always come away from a closing with more than you need to buy and fix the house. So having enough money to buy a junker isn't a problem. The problem is lining up your lender or mortgage broker to get the money for you, which you can do in a coma once you make up your mind to get it done.

How much money do you need to wholesale a house? You guessed it: nada! Well, maybe a $10 deposit to the seller. Can you raise that all by yourself? How much do you need to lease-option a house and then sublease it to a tenant-buyer? You know the answer: none!

So let's recap for a minute. Taking over "subject-to" loans on pretty houses usually requires no money from you or, at most, a small amount. Yet you can immediately lease-option a pretty house or sell with owner financing and pick up $5,000, $10,000, $20,000, or more from a deposit or down payment, all within a few days. You can also buy junkers and rehab them using private loans: getting cash when you buy and sell and never spending a dime of your own money. You can also lease-option pretty houses from the sellers and sublease to tenant-buyers, picking up deposits in the thousands within days and huge back-end checks when the buyers cash out.

And don't forget about the bargains! Flip them to bargain hunters and make $5,000, $10,000, or more and never own the house. All of this with none of your own money or credit. I don't know what's stopping you, but what stops a lot of folks is lack of grit! No guts. Afraid of their own shadow. Going through life avoiding confrontation or pain. Can't grow because they won't go. You wanna know who seems to do the best in this business? The people without money or credit but lots of grit. And, how do you get grit? Simple: You first suffer adversity and get beat up and kicked around a while. Then one day you wake up and realize no one can hurt you anymore and there's only one way to go . . . up.

When you stop worrying about losing, you can start thinking about winning. You see, people with grit have learned to stop playing not to lose and begin playing to win. Does this mean you don't have grit if you haven't been to the bottom? Of course not. Adversity is not a requirement for grit. It just seems those who are the bloodiest seem to be more fired up and move more quickly, with more passion. They've seen the black hole and they don't want to go back.

It's quite common for those who begin with money to leap before they look and spend money on stuff that doesn't produce revenue—stuff like office furniture, computers, electronics, and foolish advertising that wastes money. Smart entrepreneurs put their money in the bank and start their business on a shoestring. The fancy stuff doesn't put a dime in the bank. To do that, you must make offers, and you should be making them without using your money or your credit.

"Success seems to be connected with ACTION. Successful people keep moving. They make mistakes, but they don't quit."

Conrad Hilton

We've created a system for you to use to attract and prescreen private lenders. It's a website already set up for you where I do all the selling so all you have to do is call the lender and see how much he/she has to invest. Go to **www.RonsGoldClub.com** and enroll as a Gold member. Then when you get your password go to the membership home page and click on *"Private Lender Site"* and follow the simple instructions. You're site will be up instantly.

Pauline & Darrell- Ocala, FL

Hi Ron,

It's been awhile but that doesn't mean we haven't been doing business. We've been busy and there is always something new and exciting to learn and do!

We wanted to share our newest success story with you. We think you'll enjoy it.

We bought this log cabin from the bank for $72,000. It was a pretty expensive rehab, but it came out gorgeous. It took a little longer to sell (log cabins are hard to get financing for) than expected but even with the rehab and holding costs it was a great payday – which by the way, was today (copy of check enclosed)!!!

ASSOCIATED LAND TITLE INSURANCE OF OCALA ESCROW ACCOUNT	AMSOUTH BANK OF FLORIDA 63-468/631	89196

PAY

**One Hundred Six Thousand Five Hundred Thirty Six dollars & Eighty Four cents **

**$106,536.84

TO THE ORDER OF PD&J Properties, Inc.

VOID AFTER 90 DAYS

Betty Palmer

AUTHORIZED SIGNATURE

We made some mistakes – but hay, we learned some lessons and we still made a bunch of money!

Thanks, Ron. We never would have gotten involved in a project like this without the knowledge we gained from you. Everything from borrowing private money, having someone else do the work and even the paint and carpet colors were all things we picked up from the seminars.

Once again, a million thanks. We'll see you soon at a boot camp – we need a Ron fix!

Sincerely,

Pauline & Darrell

Pauline & Darrell

Chapter 13
How You Can Retire With An IRA Worth $1 Million

I know this sounds like another one of those glorified headlines to get your attention but without a lot of truth. I know it's a very strong statement and sounds too good to be true. But, what if it *is* true? What if you could have a cool million dollars in your IRA within a few years so you'd never have to worry about retirement income? What if you could do this without writing another check to your IRA? I have some good news and some bad news. The good news: You can! The bad news: It requires work!

Is it too much to ask you to do some work for a few years so you can retire rich? You've got to work at something anyway, so you might as well get rich while doing it. The information you're about to read is unknown to most of the world. Most people think the way to grow your IRA is to make annual contributions and let the manager of the IRA invest it in stocks and mutual funds. Then, over a period of 20 to 40 years, it grows into a large sum of money for your retirement. That's the thinking of conventional wisdom.

Let me tell you how I feel about conventional wisdom. It's almost always wrong! Let's take a look at a better way. Check it out for yourself and see if you agree. I speak to groups of people all over the country and sometimes ask how many in the room have an IRA. I have never had more than a third of the class answer yes. So, why don't more people have IRAs? Here's what they tell me:

- They can't let go of the contribution not knowing it only takes $500 to open an IRA. Having the money at hand for immediate usage is a lot more important than retirement.
- They never thought about it.
- They feel they can invest in other financial ventures that can produce more income.
- They know they should but never seem to get around to it.

If you're one of these people, it's probably time for you to wake up and take action before it's too late. You see, an IRA is about all we have left that our Uncle Sam allows us to use to grow filthy rich without paying taxes along the way. I don't have to tell you that money grows a whole lot faster if the IRS isn't taking its 25 to 40 percent share as fast as you can make it. Every dollar you send to the government is money that can't earn anything for you until the day you die. Every dollar you can stash away that's tax deferred or tax free can compound throughout the rest of your life.

For example, let's say you kept an extra $10,000 out of the IRS's hands this year and invested it at 15 percent (which you easily can), and it compounded for 20 years before you started using it. How much do you think it would grow to? How about. . . $197,155? That's about two hundred grand you could have available for retirement by wising up and keeping the ten grand you're now giving away. This is assuming you don't have to pay taxes as you go, and you don't in your IRA.

"But, Ron, my accountant tells me I can't contribute more than $6,000 each year. Where did you come up with this $10,000 figure?"

Your accountant may be right. There is a limit to how much you can contribute. But wait! Go back and ask your accountant if there is any limit on how much your IRA can make in a year from its investments. He'll scratch his head and tell you no. *There is no cap on how much income your IRA can produce!*

Incidentally, if you have the nerve, ask your accountant what his or her net worth is. I dare you! You probably won't like the answer. I want you to remember that this is the person from whom you're seeking financial advice. Also remember: The broke can't teach you how to be rich . . . they're not qualified.

"OK, Ron, so tell me how I can make my IRA wealthy without making any contributions." If you're a real estate entrepreneur, you're making money from buying and selling or keeping houses. If I've trained you, you're doing this by using little or none of your own money. The objective is to create cash and cash flow by leveraging your brain, not your wallet or credit.

And *your IRA can do the same thing,* that's right. Your IRA can buy houses, the same way you do. You have to do the work, but your IRA gets the money, tax-deferred or tax-free. Here's a real life example. A student called me with a house in Atlanta that's worth $575,000 in a gorgeous area. The seller owed $492,000 with a $4,200 per month payment. She was $13,000 in arrears. After some back and forth, she agreed to deed us the house if we made up the $13,000 in back payments.

We did our due diligence, verifying the facts and value with an appraiser. We've closed on the house and currently own it. But instead of taking title in a trust with me as beneficiary, I took title in a trust with my *IRA as beneficiary.* I had my IRA administrator send the check to the closing attorney for the back payments along with instructions on how I wanted to take title. He created the trust; I didn't even have to appear at the closing.

Now in this case, my IRA did have to come up with $13,000 to make this deal work, but normally when I get a deed, it's free or pretty close to it. Keep this in mind and don't get hung up on the down payment. Let's look at the results: We received $83,000 in equity for $13,000. We've obtained a beautiful home in the same area several Atlanta Braves have homes as well as Whitney Houston. We've purchased with no liability and can sell the same way. We simply took over the mortgage "subject-to." So what's our exit? It's simple. Sell the same way we bought it. Get as much down as possible, preferably $80,000, and deed it to someone else. Worst-case scenario is we get $40,000 or $50,000 down and take back a second. Or take something in trade. Easy in, easy out.

Let's review: If we get $80,000 and subtract $13,000 before a payment comes due, we'll net about $65,000. That's $32,500 for my partner and $32,500 for me. Whoops, that's not true; that's $32,500 for my IRA! Tax deferred. What if I did three or four of these a year? That's a hundred grand I helped my IRA earn, *tax deferred.* And we're only talking about this year. What if I did this every year until I didn't want to anymore because my IRA had more money than I could spend? You can do eight to ten deals in your IRA on an annual basis without its being called a business.

At least, this is what I've been told by the people who administer IRAs. Of course, there are a few rules and more questions. Perhaps I can't answer these questions for you, and, frankly, many accountants can't either. Seek the best advice you can find and do what you feel is best for you. Your IRA must be self-directed.

There are a few good companies we've found to handle truly self-directed IRA's. The people there understand what you're looking for, and they have taught me how to do this. Go to **www.RonLeGrand.com/Resources** and complete a self-directed IRA package. They will put your money in a money market account until you tell it what to do with the money. When you find a use for the funds, they will write the check according to your directions and mail it to the address you provide. It takes less time to carry this out than it's taken me to tell you about it.

Next, you must learn and understand the meaning of self-dealing, which can be deadly to your wealth. You cannot sell your houses to your IRA. You shouldn't get your IRA involved in any deal you or your entity was previously involved in. If your IRA buys a house, the house should go directly from the seller to the IRA and not pass through you. Don't take back notes on houses and give or sell them to your IRA. Keep it clean. Do your homework: I have a course I taped with the owner of one of these firms for real estate investors. Call *(800) 567-6128.*

Now you may be thinking I'm advocating your using your IRA money to buy houses. Not hardly. The last thing I want you to do with your IRA cash is to buy real estate. Why? Because you don't need money to buy real estate . . . and neither does your IRA.

You should buy or option deals in your IRA that don't require cash. Next, take that cash when your houses sell and buy all kinds of neat stuff to increase the yield on the cash—stuff like discounted paper, defaulted paper, mutual funds, hot stocks, and so on. Here's the point: So long as your money is tied up in real estate, it can't be getting a high return on semi-passive investments. It can only grow as fast as the real estate allows. So let's get the best of both worlds. Create cash by actively buying and selling houses with little or none of your IRA's money. Next, take those profits and make them grow by at least 15 percent per annum outside of real estate.

Roth IRAs—tax deferred or tax free. Make certain you ask about a Roth IRA and take time to learn its potential. You're never taxed, you can use it for a first-time home, and you never have to take it out. Of course, there are exceptions and rules. So take the time to learn about the Roth and use it. If you qualify I promise it will be a huge return on your time investment. I know! About now you're saying:

"Well Ron, you just told me not to use my IRA's money to buy a house, and yet you did exactly that with your own IRA."

Guilty as charged! In fact, I'm quite often guilty of actually doing the stuff I tell you about, although I actually practice what I preach! I said don't use your IRA to invest in real estate, but what I meant was *not for the long term.*

If my IRA writes a check for $13,000 to buy a house with the expectation of getting back my $13,000 plus $32,500 within 60 days, is that OK? I don't need a spread sheet on this one. That's exactly a 1,500 percent *annual* return on investment. I bet that's better than any money market or CD you currently have. I'll bet that's even better than your stock portfolio's performance last year.

Is it a great deal? Yes! Is it the best you can do? No! The best return on your money is called *infinity.* If you don't invest money, you can't measure the return. That's my kind of deal. But if you've got the cash, you've got to do something with it. So, may I be excused because I didn't get an infinity yield this time? Try to tell your accountant and banker you can get a 1,500 percent yield on your money. Watch their eyes glaze over. Remember, all it takes to get a tax-deferred, infinite yield on your IRA is for it to control or buy your real estate without using its money.

Can you option a property without money? *Yes!* Can you wholesale a house without money? Yes! Can you take a house "subject-to" without money? *Yes!* Can you lease-option a house without money? *Yes!*

Wait, here's more! Did you know your children or grandchildren can have an IRA you can start without their knowledge that can become their own when they come of age? What a way for you to provide for your children's educational future. Without writing a check! Without borrowing a dime! And if you open up an IRA for your children or grandchildren, I wouldn't tell them if I were you. Can you guess why?

Let's play with some numbers. Suppose you can set aside enough time away from your job to do three or four deals a year, netting a total of $50,000. Then you decided you were going to do the same thing for the next five years and then quit. You know you can get a 15 percent return in your sleep. Simply make loans to other investors in your city, as I discussed in the last chapter, and charge 15 percent interest. Add two or three points and maybe a prepayment penalty when it's paid off and your yield could easily top 25 percent. What was your total contribution? Zero! Your IRA made money, but you didn't contribute any of it.

What is your IRA worth at 15 percent in:

5 Years?	$387,548
10 Years?	$779,948
15 Years?	$1,567,869

OK, let's now suppose you get a little ambitious and do better deals that make $100,000 each year in your IRA.

What is your IRA worth at 15 percent in:

5 Years?	$775,069
10 Years?	$1,558,996
15 Years?	$3,135,798

Remember, I'll put $32,500 in my IRA on this deal. If you're an active real estate entrepreneur, it's no big thing to let your IRA have a few of your deals. Most people spend more time buying a car, planning a vacation, or taking in a football game, than planning for retirement. So, what about you? Is this going to be a scanned-over chapter to be quickly cast aside because your favorite TV show is about to air? Or could it be a valuable piece of information that will have a major impact on your future because you decided to take action? Hey! I'm only the messenger boy. My job is done. Yours is next.

Do you remember Marco's big option deal that netted him $2,450,000? His total cash outlay was $100. What if he had let his IRA put up the $100 and do the option instead of him? That means . . . he'd have had $2,450,000 in his Roth IRA tax free for life. Had he simply put that money into mutual funds earning an average annual return of 12 percent (which is easy to get), his IRA would be worth:

- ♦ $ 8,085,948 in 10 years
- ♦ $14,689,714 in 15 years
- ♦ $78,163,529 in 29 years (his retirement age of 59 1/2)

Not bad for a $100 investment, huh? Bad news! Marco didn't use his IRA. Oh well! What's an extra $78 million? Nothing he can do now but make it up on the next one.

Caution. The example I just used involves buying property that comes with debt financing. Even though you or your IRA didn't create the debt, the IRS may still consider the purchase debt related. This could trigger UBIT (unrelated business income tax) and cause the transaction to be taxed on its profit.

UBIT can easily be eliminated by using an option instead of a purchase. Have your IRA option the property from the seller or even from a land trust if done correctly. A little time learning the rules is time well spent. In fact, it's worth a *tax-free* fortune to you.

This subject is of extreme importance to your retirement and peace of mind, and I'm on a mission to educate America about this valuable information. If you have interest call my office at (800) 567-6128 and tell them you're reading this book and I said to cut the $497 cost in half for you. That's $249.

You're Welcome!

"The secret of success is to be ready for opportunity when it comes and then take action before it leaves."

Ron LeGrand®

Part Three

Legal Considerations

Chapter 14
Land Trusts And Legal Considerations

Are you aware that every time you sign your name on a note, you're risking everything you own to fulfill that debt? Did you know that in most states creditors can sue for default on a mortgage note and come after you personally without even bothering with the house? That's their right. They can look to all your other assets to satisfy your debt in place of, or in addition to, the property you mortgaged.

But, don't worry! I have a solution to that problem for some types of financing. This solution also solves several other problems associated with owning real estate. It's simple, yet it's extremely important to all of us who buy houses. Anyone can use it, and it doesn't cost a nickel extra to take advantage of it. This solution is called a *land trust*. First, let's learn what it is and then I'll do a crash course on why and how to use it.

➤ *Definition Of A Land Trust*

It's irrelevant to us, as investors, how land trusts originated or that a lot of history is behind them. Such trusts were first used hundreds of years ago, but we only need to focus on how they can benefit us now.

For simplicity, consider the land trust a method of taking title to property nothing more, nothing less. It is an agreement between the *officer* of the trust, called the *trustee*, and the person who actually controls the property, called the *beneficiary*. The trust identifies certain duties that each agrees to perform. The agreement is signed by both parties, and then it becomes the property of the beneficiary. The beneficiary owns the trust, and the trust owns the property. The trustee has only those powers granted to him or her by the beneficiary, and he or she performs minimal duties—usually just signing the documents. The trustee has no personal liability or responsibility to do anything more than those minimal tasks.

A land trust has two main components: The first and most important is the *deed to a trust,* which replaces a regular deed and includes the language that both sets up the trust as soon as the deed is recorded and gives the trustee limited powers; the second component is the *trust agreement,* which spells out all the conditions of the trust. This agreement stays with you and is the only document that discloses the beneficial interest. Both documents are easy to complete and not a big deal.

People ask me all the time: *"How do I form a land trust?"* Simple! Fill out the deed to a trust and record it. You've just funded the trust with the property, so your trust is formed. It exists until the term stated in the trust agreement expires or until you deed the property from the trust to someone else.

➢ Reasons To Use A Land Trust

Savvy investors use land trusts every day. This powerful document offers personal and legal advantages not associated with any other kind of property ownership. I'll discuss each of the benefits briefly in the following sections.

PRIVACY

Secrecy is an important aspect of a trust. No one knows you are the beneficiary except for you and the trustee. When somebody checks the title to the property, you don't own the property; in fact, you have no interest in the property as far as the rest of the world knows. All they see is that the property is owned by a trust. They don't know the beneficiary's name. The only way they will find that out is by court order, or if your trustee has a big mouth.

A deed is recorded at the courthouse and bears the name of the trustee as grantee. Nowhere does it mention the beneficiary's name. The trust document itself remains in the possession of the beneficiary. It isn't recorded anywhere nor does it become public knowledge. Therefore, you have total privacy.

LOAN LIABILITY

The trust can and should be used to create seller carryback financing. There is absolutely no reason for you to ever personally sign a note to a seller. If you fail to heed this advice, you may very well be headed for an expensive real-world "seminar."

The process is simple. The trust takes title to the house, so the trustee signs the note as trustee. Because your name appears nowhere on the document, you are therefore not personally liable. So long as the words *as trustee* appear after the trustee's signature, he or she is not liable either. Presto! You have just created a note that won't ever come back to haunt you. The most the seller can get back is the property because you didn't guarantee the debt, the trust did, and the only asset in the trust is the one house you bought from the seller. So in effect, the house guarantee is the debt.

LAWSUIT PROTECTION

Another key reason to use a land trust is limited lawsuit protection. It's not a foolproof plan to keep you from being sued because your beneficial interest can be attached, but it's a lot better than owning property in your own name. The first thing an attorney does to prepare to sue you is check your assets; all the attorney can do with a land trust is check your name. But if your name doesn't show up, and it won't, the attorney doesn't have a clue you have anything to do with this property.

The only way the attorney can find out is to get wind of the fact that you own properties in trust, call you in for a deposition, and ask you point blank, "Do you own any interest in any trusts?" At that time, you have to either answer yes or commit perjury. Let's assume, however, that you leave your properties titled in your own name or, even worse, jointly with your spouse. Now you get sued, and the plaintiff (the suer) is awarded a large judgment over and above your insurance benefits. The minute that judgment is recorded, it attaches to your properties and prevents any future sale or refinancing until the judgment is satisfied, if ever. In fact, the plaintiff can now start action to attach your assets, and everything you worked for is lost.

On the other hand, let's say your properties were in a land trust before the legal action started. First of all, a name search will produce nothing because you own nothing as far as public records are concerned. This alone will stop most lawsuits in their tracks. If it is obvious a judgment can't be collected if won, it would be fruitless for anyone to pursue a lawsuit and incur the costs unless insurance proceeds were available. Under those circumstances, the case would usually be settled out of court.

But let's assume none of that happens but you are sued anyway, and the suer gets a judgment. It doesn't attach to the properties because you don't own them. The trust owns the house, and you own the trust.

Before we become too smug, be aware that this legal protection doesn't prevent a good attorney from coming after your interest in the trust. But the attorney must first discover you have an interest and then that there's someone willing to pay the high cost of another separate, expensive, and risky legal action. Even though it's not a foolproof lawsuit protector, a trust sure beats owning property in your own name.

ESTATE PLANNING

A land trust is a good first step to estate planning, but it is by no means a total plan. Many kinds of trusts and other entities are available.

If your property is in a trust and you die, whoever is your beneficiary now owns the trust. He or she now owns whatever interest you owned. To avoid probate, however, in most cases this needs to be taken a step further. The most widely used method is to place the land trust in a living trust or a family limited partnership. And, this topic could lead us into a discussion that would fill a book so big you'd have to haul it around in a wheelbarrow.

ATTACHMENT OF JUDGMENTS AND LIENS

I just discussed lawsuit protection as a result of the privacy created by using a land trust, but consider this:

You just got a huge tax bill from the IRS because you didn't pay all your taxes two years ago, and the IRS didn't agree with your version of the return. Several months go by, but you just can't come up with the money to pay and the IRS issues a tax lien against you. As soon as the lien is recorded, you now have a lien on every piece of property you own in your name. You've just become the "stuckee." You can't sell or refinance until the IRS is paid.

Had your properties been titled in a land trust, as they should be, the lien wouldn't attach to the properties. Remember, you don't own them; the land trust does. *A lien against you can't attach to assets you don't own.* You may sell some properties to get the money, or you may do nothing. Your options are still available because you made a very simple move to never own anything on public record in your own name.

For clarity, I didn't say the IRS can't get your assets; I merely said the lien doesn't automatically attach on recordation. If the IRS wants your beneficial interests in the land trusts, it'll get them. But, chances are good they never will. The odds are with you, but don't construe a land trust as some kind of tax-avoidance device. It's a transparent entity so far as the IRS is concerned, which means the IRS will tax you in the entity you report ownership on your return, regardless of whether title is in your name or a land trust.

If I were you, the IRS is one gorilla I wouldn't dance with. The good news about paying taxes is there's plenty left over for you. If you're worried about paying too much in taxes . . . *you ain't makin' enough money.*

EASE OF TRANSFER

When you sell to buyers who understand trusts, quite often they would prefer you assign them the trust rather than having the trust deed the property to them. This action saves closing costs because nothing changes at the courthouse. The trust still owns the house, and you are simply selling the trust. It is done with one sheet of paper called an *assignment of beneficial interest*. It's as simple as your signing it, your trustee signing it, and you're handing it to a buyer. That's it! Now, of course, your buyer will want to check the title first and will probably want someone to prepare a closing statement, but all the normal transfer and recording costs have been avoided.

Bank loans. When you go to a bank to borrow money that is secured by property, the bank will require your personal signature on the note. It will not let you take title in the trust because the bank doesn't understand it. If you have intentions of buying a property and refinancing, don't take title in the name of the trust. A bank won't make a loan to a trust. If you are going to refinance, take title in your name, refinance, and *then* place the property in a trust. The lender cannot call the loan due as long as you are the controlling interest in the trust, even if the loan contains a due-on-sale clause. In 1982, the Garn-St. Germaine Federal Depository Institution Act made it illegal for a lender to call a loan simply because property has been transferred into a trust.

➢ Appointing A Trustee

The trustee must be a person you trust or in many states it can be your corporation or limited liability company (LLC). You could make a family member, friend, or title agent your trustee. The trustee can be someone out of state, but remember that the trustee does the signing for any transactions of the trust. The trustee can close deals for you when you're not in town because of the trust provisions. But, the trustee can sign documents only because you, as beneficiary, give him or her permission. The beneficiary has all the control. The trustee has no control, except to do what the beneficiary instructs; the trustee signs all documents at the direction of the beneficiary.

This has been a brief introduction to a few of the key ideas regarding the use of trusts. To use trusts effectively you need to learn much more, but the subject is too extensive for this book. I have thousands of students using land trusts nationwide. That's because trusts are simple to use, cost nothing extra, and provide all the benefits previously discussed. Bearing that in mind, please don't let a so-called expert convince you otherwise. Get the facts from the people who know instead of constantly reinventing the wheel.

If you buy real estate, you should be using land trusts! It's just that simple.

➢ *Ignorance Warning*

You will meet resistance from people about land trusts, especially attorneys who don't understand them. If you need an attorney's blessing before you use one, the chances aren't good you'll find an attorney to give you that blessing.

The problem: Attorneys just don't get it, and they confuse it with other business entities like business trusts that require a tax return, ID number, and bank account. A land trust needs none of those things. It needs:

- ◆ No tax ID #
- ◆ No tax return
- ◆ No annual dues
- ◆ No bank account
- ◆ No special forms to file
- ◆ No permission from untrained advisors or anyone else on earth

Some attorneys attempt to nix its use because there is no state statute covering land trusts. Therefore, attorneys assume it can't be used and come to other erroneous conclusions derived from ignorance or lack of research.

Absence of evidence is not evidence of absence.

No harm will come to you if you use a land trust, but serious harm can come if you don't. Let's look at a worst-case scenario. You put your house in a land trust and someone convinces you you've done an evil thing and must take it back out.

It's simple. Fill out a deed from the trust to you and go to your recorder's office and record it. Voilà! No more land trust. Back to normal with your asset exposed to creditors and predators and a sitting duck for anyone with a smarter lawyer than yours.

If I were you, I'd be very careful listening to anyone who suggests to you that exposing your assets is the right thing to do.

Who are you listening to?

"Each problem has hidden in it an opportunity so powerful that it literally dwarfs the problem. The greatest success stories were created by people who recognized a problem and turned it into an opportunity."

Joseph Sugarman

Part Four

Success

Chapter 15
Tigers Are The Last To Starve In The Jungle

In light of the 9/11 tragedies in New York and Washington, D.C., I thought it would be good to talk about mental toughness. I got a few letters asking me what I thought would happen to the real estate market after the attack of 9/11. Tons of these letters were written in fear. Folks were afraid that business would take a dive because the market is afraid to buy houses, and everything will change. Here's a news flash: It absolutely has changed!

The world will never be the same. We'll all be more afraid of lunatics now than we were before September 11. Security has tightened, and everyone is talking about it. The news is a 24-hour talk about terrorists, and no one is certain what they'll do next. But one thing is certain: People will always need a place to live. I remember when the prime rate was 18 percent in the early 1980s; back then I had my hands full buying houses from people who couldn't sell. I spent my time helping people find a way to sell to me!

The Realtors® were falling like flies, and everyone was bad mouthing real estate because you couldn't make a living at it, at least that was the gossip going around. I was too hungry to listen to that baloney, so I bought about 70 houses that year! I guess everyone forgot to tell me how bad the market was— either that or I wasn't listening. Frankly, back then I did a whole lot less listening than I do now.

Today the prime rate is low. It would seem as if sellers could find buyers as fast as they put a house on the market. Here's another news flash:

Houses don't sell any faster or slower whether the prime rate is 2 percent or 6 percent.

It ain't the rate that sells the houses. It's the person in

charge of making the sale. Oh sure, lower payments help, but a positive attitude and a friendly voice help a lot more. That was the case in 1982 and it's the case now.

Your attitude will make you wealthy or it will make you a whiner!

If you think anything terrorists can do will destroy the need for Americans to own a home or ruin your business as a real estate entrepreneur, perhaps you should get away from the TV and get back to reality! To be blunt, I'd suggest you grow up and quit listening to all the dream stealers who are looking to blame others for their own failures.

Some people ask me if I am afraid to get on planes now, and my answer is absolutely not. I didn't get where I am today by sticking my head in the sand and letting lunatics run my life! I couldn't wait to get back on a plane. I look at it like this: I've got a better chance of getting killed in my car than on a plane, and that is a proven statistic. So, I guess you could say the odds are in my favor. Besides, can you think of a safer time to fly than now? Security is at an all-time high, and no plane full of American men will let terrorists take it down since we can guess their true intentions now. I'd be more afraid of having my lifestyle disrupted because I'm filled with fear or because I lost my freedom or health.

Prostate and colon cancer along with heart disease scare me a whole lot more than a lunatic with a death wish. I fear stagnation, procrastination, laziness, and paralysis and don't give a second thought to the morons. I don't sit around wondering who's going to take my assets. I don't spend more time playing not to lose than playing to win. My assets are protected, and frankly they're not all that important to me anymore. I could lose them all tomorrow, and I would have them back in a year! At least the ones I'd want back!

My biggest asset besides my family is located between my ears and it's not my nose! That asset took 65 years to develop, and as long as I have it, money isn't hard to come by. If you take a look around and ask yourself what really has meaning in your life, I bet you'll discover it isn't anything you've bought.

Willie Mays said it best:

"It's not my wife . . . it's not my life . . . why worry?"

I guess it all comes down to your attitude, but far too many people worry about things that don't mean spit! The worse violators worry about things they can't change or control. What good will it do to sit around and fret? Get busy. Do something positive. Go make some offers and sell some houses!

If you're busy enough, you won't have time to worry. Get away from the doom and the gloom and turn off the TV for a while. Get to some of my events and get recharged! Hang around people on the move and get away from those who can't talk about anything but what's on the news. Some suggestions:

- **Go make some money!**
- **Donate to charities!**
- **Go back to church if it's been a while!**

Do something new, such as buying a car or taking a vacation . . . on a plane! See some new places and make some new friends. Join a new club or volunteer for a political office. Write a speech or a book! Hug your children and take them to a movie. Sit down and talk with them for one hour with no interruptions. Go to a party or, better yet, have one! Invite the neighbors over! Take your spouse to a new restaurant and buy the most expensive thing on the menu, then go home and make love until morning!

Go shopping and get a new wardrobe. Have some of your clothes made by a tailor. Get a massage and a full body treatment. Have the masseuse come to your home every week. Hire someone to mow your lawn so you can sell your lawnmower! Next time you're in the grocery store, look for someone who needs assistance and offer to pay for his or her groceries.

Volunteer to serve food to the homeless on the holidays. Put up the biggest Christmas display in your life! Have a flagpole put in your front yard and fly the biggest American flag it can hold. Forget about all the stuff that can go wrong and think about making things go right.

Focus on what you can control and forget about the things you can't. Develop mental toughness! Picture yourself filthy stinking rich and work every day to make it happen. Pretty soon it *will* happen. Then you can show someone else how to and become that someone else's hero.

Enjoy every moment of life you have left and don't let others use your time unless you're willing to give it up. Cherish every moment and never stop asking yourself: Is this the best use of my time? If you maintain control, mental toughness will come. If you let others control your emotions, you'll be a weak, mental wreck, and no good to yourself or anyone else.

Toughen up, grow up and move up!

Join the ranks of the mentally tough by making mistakes and living with them knowing its all part of learning. You can't get tough without getting beaten up first. That means you must always be moving forward, not standing still.

Find out what's broke and fix it. If you're not making enough money, the only possible reason is looking at you from the other side of the mirror. Accept responsibility for your own actions and toughen up. It's you, baby! All you and nobody else! It isn't me, and it isn't the family or the boss, it's *you!!*

The quicker you accept that fact, the quicker you can begin fixing you. The terrorists didn't make you who you are, and they certainly can't keep you from doing what you want to do.

Sorry to be so brutal, but frankly I have had a bad day listening to whiners looking for excuses, so I'm taking it out on you. Guess I should get a little more mental toughness huh?

"Failure is not an option. It's just the nagging

possibility that helps you stay focused."

Anonymous

Ron,

Hi my name is Brad Witzel. I am from Chattanooga, TN and I am seventeen years old. I attended the seminar in Chattanooga where you spoke a month or two back. I had just finished reading one of your books and I was (and still am) on fire about real estate investing. After hearing about me by word of mouth, a man called me and told me that he had a vacant house for sell that his mother gave to him free and clear. He told me that he wanted $25,000 for the house that needed quite a bit of work. We spoke for a few minutes and I found out that he was very motivated because the house that he was living in was about to be foreclosed on. I then asked him "if I paid cash and closed quickly what would be the least you would take?" He told me that he would take $15,000 if I hurried up. I then made an appointment and looked at the house. While at the house I told him that I could not give him the $15,000 because the house was in such disrepair. I offered him $10,000 and after thinking about it for a moment he accepted. We signed the contract that day. I now have two men doing the work for me. I am going to put $18,000 in it and I will have no problem selling it for $52,000 for a profit of $24,000! I expect that I will have it sold in February sometime. Better than working at a fast food restaurant huh?

Thanks a lot,
Brad Witzel

Chapter 16

You Can't Eat Everything That Looks Appetizing

Here's my checklist to determine when to say no to opportunity. Perhaps, it will help you do the same if you alter it to fit your lifestyle.

Opportunity Checklist

1. **Will it require an investment of my money that I don't have or am not willing to invest at this time?**

If it does it's an easy NO unless I can come up with the money elsewhere and like the deal enough to do so.

2. **Is it worth the investment of money, time and resources or am I doing it simply because I can?**

In my case if it's a commercial property it must have a profit in the millions that we can get at within the next three years. I'm not a land speculator nor do I buy buildings so we can do all the work and break even. I'd rather go fishing and skip the grief.

3. **Is it a high risk venture or do I have several exit strategies in mind that are reasonable and will produce good profit with bad numbers?**

If it's high risk out of my control, I'm out. If it's in my control I can always find a way. If everything has to work out perfectly to win, I'm out. It never does. Always takes much longer and costs more. Murphy is my buddy. If my plan one doesn't work, what's plan two and three? Better be a good answer or I'm gone.

4. **Is the opportunity exciting or boring?**

With so much to do, why do things that you dread? I'm not too old to have fun. I want to brag a little about my accomplishments. How you gonna brag about boring stuff unless you hang around boring people and I don't. To me real estate developments and resorts and restaurants and teaching and oil and learning are exciting. The stock market, sightseeing, gambling and the evening news are boring. But that's just me. Told you I wasn't normal.

5. **Is the opportunity something I have even the remotest familiarity with or totally out of my expertise?**

Learning about new business while you're vested or invested in making it successful can be a painful experience. I won't say I don't do things I don't know, cause I do. I know very little about restaurants, oil and other ventures. But, my solution to this problem is simple.

I Find The Smartest Experts I Can And Make Them My Partner.

They know the ropes so I don't have to, if I trust them (and if I don't they aren't a partner). Sometimes it doesn't work out, but I know there's always another expert available on anything I do.

I've turned down numerous opportunities I was clueless on and didn't know an expert. Some seemed very lucrative. I don't regret any. Of course, I don't know what I missed either.

I've learned to say no quickly if it doesn't meet the above criteria. Some people get themselves all bogged down in worthless projects that aren't worth doing even if they work out well. The same attitude should apply to all the houses you do as well. Focus on the deals that will make you a lot of money and don't let the time waster drag you into a manucia trap. It doesn't take any more time to do a rehab that makes $50,000 than one that does $20,000. A pretty house deal with $50,000 in equity is the exact same process to acquire as one with $10,000 equity. A wholesale deal that makes you $25,000 is not much harder to find than a $5,000 deal.

You should see the big pile of letters we get from students with checks over $100,000!

Ask any of them how they feel about selecting the high

paying opportunities over the low paying. I think you get the message. It's about quality, not quantity. When someone brags to me about doing 5-10 deals a month, I always wonder how much money they produce. That's all that counts.

"The biggest difference between an average income and financial freedom is... implementation."

Bill Glazer

Gary Hardoerfer & MaryAnn Deatherage-Jacksonville, FL

Dear Ron,

On January 27th we completed our first deal since attending the QTRE Boot Camp in Chicago Nov 28 through Dec 3. We got a house under contract for $38,000 and wholesaled it to another investor for $49,000 and closed on it yesterday. We did an assignment and got a check for $11,000. It was a heck of a lot easier than rehabbing a house.

We've been listening to your tapes and CD's for years. I was listening to one of your CD's last summer and heard you say "if you don't attend a Boot Camp, you are missing 70% of the information" and right then, I called to sign up for boot camp. Wow, how true statement was. We learned enough in the first 2 hours to pay for the entire boot camp. We were blow away with the many ways to work the business. We purchased programs from the Wolfs, Kathy Kennebrook, and Ben Pargman.

We decided after the boot Camp we were going to crank up our buying machine and we have done everything we were told to do. The leads are coming into PatLive like crazy. We can't even keep up with them.

Here's a snapshot of what else we currently have going on:

- One Feb1st we close on our first short sale The bank discounted the seller's loan from $139,000 to $100,000 and we wholesaled for $112,000 to another investor and we will net $10,000
- We have 5 other short sales in the works and are using Ben Pargman's Short Sale Service to negotiate the deals.
- We have the deeds to (2) "subject-to" houses which we will be taking over soon.
- We have 1 other wholesale deal in the works which will net us $5,000.
- We closed on Jan 30 on a rehab we completed and sold and will net us $25,000. We have 2 rehabs for sale now, 3 that are almost finished and ready to sell, and 2 more under contract to purchase in Feb.
- On one of the rehabs a person called our "Houses Wanted" ad. We bought the house for $22,000, the ARV is $135,000. We will net over $35,000 on the deal

From the deals above we will net somewhere between $400,000 and $500,000! Our goal is $1,000,000 in net profit for the year. We are so excited about this business and thank you for your tools and programs to help us succeed.

Warmest regards,

Gary Hardoerfer & MaryAnn Deatherage

Chapter 17
It's Not My Fault

A while back, I hired a full-time mechanic to work on my jet to reduce the maintenance costs and improve its reliability. He was sitting in my office with my pilot, my CFO and myself and we carefully and slowly pointed out to him all the reasons he should incorporate to save money and provide more asset protection.

I told him I'd put him on a salary if he insisted, but it'd cost him a lot of money in lost deductions and other benefits and there was really no reason not to incorporate. Of course, that would mean he'd have to make tax deposits and file one more tax return each year to save at least $10,000 in taxes he's currently paying. I even volunteered my CFO to handle the tax deposits for him.

The next morning, my mechanic called and said he decided he'd rather be an employee. This corporation stuff was just too much to handle and it kept him awake at night. He just couldn't deal with the idea of doing anything new or different to improve his financial position in life, which obviously sucked.

Actually, it didn't surprise me at all and I expected his answer to be exactly what it was. When he gets too old to work and applies for social security, his net worth will be approximately what it was the day he was born.

Why? Because He Won't Accept Responsibility For His Own Actions And Do What It Takes To Effect Positive Change.

Unfortunately, that's exactly how 95% of the population reacts and why only 5% are in the high income, high wealth bracket. I hope you're one of the 5%.

The opposite of this story is my pilot, Don, whom I accidentally found because his wife works at Global Publishing. He works for Delta and has several thousand hours in the cockpit. I know he'll be reading this, so I have to be careful what I say, but I think he'll agree with my assessment of his situation.

You see, he has one big problem—he's a thinker brain. I'm glad he is. All pilots should be. The world needs thinker brains to keep us reptile brains in check. But his analytical personality tends to make him over analyze and spend more time on what can go wrong than what can go right. It takes him five times more facts and time to make a decision than it does me.

In spite of this handicap, he's bought his first investment house with no money and over $50,000 in equity. He simply got the deed after a seller called him on an ad. The house needed $15,000 in work, which he finally got completed about 3 ½ months after buying the house. That's right, 3 ½ months for a job that should take two weeks max.

But hey, it's his first deal and first experience with contractors so I'll cut him some slack. He'll still do well because he bought right. No money down, no personal liability, and a lot of equity on a well-located house. Give him a round of applause.

I'll keep you posted when he sells the house, which will probably be about a year from now. Just kidding Don. I know it won't take a day over six months to move that house.

I'm told there are two people you shouldn't insult—your cook, and your pilot, who has your life in his hands.

Seriously, kudos to Don for being bold enough to make that first move. In his world of thinker brain pilots, he gets criticized for even trying. In spite of that, he's slowly overcoming his fears and pushing forward to his first real estate success, then his second and his third until one day, not too far off, he'll be making more money than the CEO of Delta, and maybe even hiring his own pilot.

The difference between Don and the mechanic is Don is moving forward and the mechanic has his head in the sand. Don has accepted the responsibility and the reality that everything that happens to him, good or bad, is his fault.

I'm presently twenty pounds overweight. I don't like it.

My pants don't fit right. My belt's too tight. It drains my energy and causes back pain sometimes if I stay in bed too long—not to mention it distorts my manly physique and puts a strain on my heart.

Then, you might ask, why are you overweight?
The Answer! I Eat Too Much Crap And Won't Exercise My Fat Ass.

Actually, I think I should sue the fast food restaurants for serving me that crap. They should know their food makes people fat and the harm they're causing to society. It's all their fault...or not!

I know why I'm fat and how to fix it. It's simple...eat less, move more. When I want to bad enough, you may consider me skinny.

I also know that every business problem I incur is also my fault and if I contract a disease of some sort, it's also my fault, most likely from the crap I eat. No one to blame but myself.

Ok Ron, What's The Point?

If your business is not going the way you like, there's a reason.

It Ain't Lack Of Opportunity.

If you are not in the financial position you'd like to be, it is **NOT** because of a shortage of opportunity. You need to get that out of your head.

Opportunity is all around you, and my world is fully populated with people who started from scratch, from zero or worse than zero, and quickly created large income, successful businesses and wealth in a dizzying short time from real estate investing to sales to speaking to direct marketing to you name it. In fact, there are so many ways to start from zero and do well financially, the only real reasons to stay poor are ignorance, laziness, or habit.

That'll sound harsh to anyone reading this who is poor.

This is not to suggest I have no empathy for people in financial trouble or who are poor. I've been both. And, I recognize there are people who legitimately have never had exposure to the very idea of possibilities to do better, and that is a societal problem we ought to address differently than we do. But I doubt you're in that category. If you're reading this book, odds are, you aren't that deprived and ignorant. You aren't an illiterate third generation welfare dependent who has never been outside the ghetto. You know better. And if you know it is possible to do well, rather than doing poorly and being disappointed about it, demands action. Not acceptance of failure.

If you're not doing well in real estate, or any business, here's a list of reasons why. Of course, you may be saying, "I couldn't possibly know why you're not doing well and it's none of my business." You'd be wrong on both accounts. Your problems are no different than those I've helped students solve for years now and helping you get rich is my business.

You Wanna Know A Secret?

It's not really that hard! You're half way there now because you've already cracked the code to success.

If You Want To Get Rich, You Must First Put Yourself In A Position To Do So.

You've done that. You're a real estate entrepreneur or an internet marketer or both, or about to be. You've found your vehicle. Now all you have to do is put it in drive and give it gas and let no S.O.B. stop you. Back to the list of reasons that will stop you from doing well:

1. **Not generating enough leads.** Do the yellow letter campaigns exactly like I laid it out or call some FSBOs and see what happens. It does not matter where you live.

2. **Wasting leads.** This is a training problem easily fixed by attending our training events. Don't attend, waste leads. Do attend, make a fortune. One half of one deal pays for all this. You've lost that much this week. Check your trash can. The art of prescreening is critical. You must learn it

quickly or face extinction. Once you learn it, one hour a week prescreening leads will drive a million dollar business. Until you learn it, a million dollar business will drive you twenty hours a week or more, wasting production time.

3. **Simply won't go get the contract signed, even when you can.** This is a fear problem that can be fixed with persistence and a little grit. Get off your ass and go see the sellers you've prescreened and get the contract. The paperwork will be wrong, you'll say the wrong things, talk too much, make a mess, and then discover nobody cares.

4. **You're getting deals but having trouble selling fast enough.** Again, this is a training problem. Get to our classes and learn how to sell on autopilot. Get the biggest problem out of the way...YOU. Let our system work. Quit fighting it because you think you can do it better. Maybe you can, but if the roof is leaking, you don't wait until it caves in to fix it. Put my system in place first, then make it better. Then you'll discover you don't need to improve on a system that sells houses faster than you ever can.

♦ If you're talking to buyers before they've seen the house and been prescreened, you're doing it wrong and making a mess. It's **Your Fault.**

♦ If you're showing houses, you need therapy. It's **Your Fault.**

♦ If you're not getting enough leads, you're lazy. It's **Your Fault.**

♦ Fix this part of your business and the biggest time waster of all has been slain.

♦ Take a trip where you can think and analyze what the real problem is and go to work on the solutions. They're really not hard to find and implement.

Ask yourself this...
Has Anyone Else In My Area Ever Had The Same Problems And Overcome Them?

"There are risks and costs to a program of action. But they are far less than the long-range risks and costs of comfortable inaction."

John Fitzgerald Kennedy

David Grace-Jacksonville, FL

Dear Ron,

I am writing to thank you for the help I have received by participating in your Mentoring Program. For me it was the missing link between learning the basics at Boot Camps and being able to apply all that material to begin making deals. I had previously attended the Quick Turn Real Estate School, went home and did nothing with the material. At that time the Mentoring Program was not available, or if it was, I as unaware of it. More than a year went by when I received an email from your office about a webinar you were about to give describing your program to help students who had trouble getting started. I listened to it and immediately knew it was for me. When I enrolled in the Mentoring Program I was assigned Jon and Stephanie Iannotti as my mentors.

This was an excellent match for me and I consider myself fortunate for this match up. Their knowledge and experience in both teaching and doing transactions was very evident from the start, but they never made me feel dumb or inadequate. I can't say enough about them. They were always available and I never once had trouble getting in touch or getting the information I was after. They shared everything they had without hesitation and I hope we stay in touch for a long, long time. The time for my six month mentorship has ended recently. Your Mentorship Program was all I anticipated. It really did fill the in the detail s of my learning in the Boot Camps, CD's and home study systems.

I live in the Boston area and I used Yellow Letters primarily to generate my leads and have closed 2 deals. They were both wholesale deals and I have included photos of both of them. I also have 3 short sale deals in progress. The profit from the 2 transactions I have closed on have paid for the entire cost of the Mentor Program *plus* all I have spent on marketing with the Yellow Letters and taking the incoming calls using virtual assistants for the entire 6 months of the program.

Ron, I am glad you have made the Mentorship Program and Jon and Stephanie Iannotti available to me; otherwise I would still be paralyzed with fear and inaction.

Many thanks,

David Grace

Chapter 18
Do You Have The Courage To Be Rich?

I'm constantly amazed at how the majority of the human race in a great country like America would rather spend their entire life being mediocre, swapping hours for dollars, taking little risk, playing not to lose, than going for the gusto and getting everything possible out of the short time we have on this earth.

Is It Fun To Be You?

If the answer is no, what are you gonna do about it? Will your life continue to be mediocre and boring, or will you gain some guts and go for the gusto? Is winning big more important to you than surviving?

Do You Have The Courage To Become Filthy Stinking Rich?

Look, I was a mechanic who barely cleared high school. No money, no credit, no training, no rich relatives, and no simple plan to follow to success. It was a tough struggle where I invented the steps incurring much pain, but I enjoyed almost every day of the struggle. I only have one regret....

Why Did It Have To Take So Damn Long?

You're so lucky! What took me twenty years to figure out has been put in an aerosol can so you can simply spray on success almost overnight. With the easy to follow and simple plan I've created over the years, you get to bypass those twenty years, and make it happen in one.

Assuming, of course, you possess a few key ingredients:

1. You want to! If you don't, I can't help you.
2. You'll follow the simple steps and do what you're told. Since that ain't likely, I'll settle for <u>most</u> of what you're told.
3. You'll keep doing it until you fix what <u>you</u> broke, and put it on auto-pilot.

4.   You currently possess, or somehow acquire enough guts (courage) to get the job done no matter what SOB tries to stop you, and they will. Some even have your last name.

When I started, I didn't have much to work with, but I did have one thing I wouldn't swap for money: **GUTS**.

Over the years, I think I've discovered what causes the gutlessness disease. I believe it's low self-esteem caused by very little success in one's life, or success followed by failure. This low self-esteem can only be cured by one thing: a series of small successes leading to larger success.

The only evidence of progress will be in the form of checks, followed by more checks until gutlessness is a thing of the past. You can listen to Tony Robbins tapes until your ears bleed, but without proof it will all pass quickly. **Show Me The Money!**

Here's An Absolute Certainty...
It's Easier To Develop Courage When You Ain't Broke.

Cash flow is king! When you can pay your bills, blow money on frivolous things, and still have plenty left over, you get to play to win, not spend your life playing not to lose. You don't need a million bucks to live and feel like a millionaire. You need strong cash flow, and I'd suggest you get it quickly... 'cause you can.

However, that doesn't mean you should spend every dime you get your hands on. If you want to buy all the junk you dream about, go ahead, as long as paying for it doesn't mean a zero bank balance at the end of the month.

Get your cash flow up and there isn't much you want you can't afford. You can buy a $2,000,000 home, a $100,000 car for husband and wife, a boat, and live high on the hog for an outgo of less than $20,000 a month. If your income is $50,000 a month and a third of that goes to taxes, you still have a lot left over.

Now get your income to $75,000 a month and you'll feel

like the king of the hill, and any past low self-esteem problems are fixed for life.

So, you think that sounds far-fetched for you, eh?

Well, it won't be if you have a little courage and decide you're worthy. Why is it okay for other people to get rich and not you? Are they any better or smarter than you? Do they deserve it more? Or, could it be they just have more **GUTS?**

Seventy-five thousand dollars a month is only $900,000 a year. I know Realtors®, mortgage brokers, contractors, and carpet cleaners that make more than that. Show me a profession and I'll show you someone making a million or more per year with a lot less work with than real estate that produces checks from $50,000 to $500,000 per deal and more. And that's residential. Don't even get me started on commercial, where the smallest deal I'll do has a minimum net of $2,000,000.

If you break down the $900,000 target and adapt it to your personal plan, market and guts level, it should be easy to see it's only a handful of deals per year; and that doesn't include any other income you have such as your job, your spouse's job and other business.

It's Just Simple Math!

If you're reading this and you haven't done your first deal yet, you may be trying to justify why it doesn't apply to you.

Sorry, that dog won't hunt. It does apply to you if you want to get rich. Every successful real estate millionaire began with their first deal. You ain't no different.

If you haven't done number one yet, there's only a handful of reasons why:

1. **You're brand new!** OK, this excuse is only good for about a month.
2. **You haven't been trained!** Why not? You know we can fix that as soon as you say so. What's stopping you? Is it money? Bull… I didn't have any and neither did thousands

of my most successful students. Is it time? Baloney! What are you doing that's more important? Making a living. Good, we need job slaves. They keep Wal-Mart in business. If you think education is expensive, try ignorance.

3. *You're Trying, But Nothing Seems To Be Happening!* So what are you doing to screw up your business, and if you don't think the problem is you, grow up and accept the fact that everything that happens to you is your fault! There are only five steps to your success, at which are you failing!

♦ **Locating Prospects**: Yellow letter, call FSBO's, or few other inexpensive or free things.
♦ **Prescreening Prospects**: A little training.
♦ **Construct And Present Offer**: The right prospects will make you an offer.
♦ **Follow Up**: Get it in writing and check title.
♦ **Sell Quickly**: A little training.

Most people who fail are dealing with suspects, not prospects, and don't really know how to tell the difference. This is easy to fix, but I can't do it in a book.

Another big mistake is not getting enough leads. That's impossible if you work the yellow letter correctly (few do). Getting leads is easy. Getting good leads is tougher because you've got to kiss a lot of frogs, and good leads are a minority. Most sellers are a waste of your time.

Gosh, there's a business revelation. You can't deal with everyone. All businesses require prescreening, and no business can deal with every suspect it obtains. Then why on earth is it such a big shock for beginners to understand all people with a house for sale are not worthy of your time?

Of course, there's another problem that lives lurking behind the scenes of some (far too many) of my well-intentioned, most deserving students... **gutlessness!**

Locating the prospects, prescreening them and building

a stack of leads two feet deep won't replace a lack of guts.

Do You Have The Courage To Be Rich?

If so, is it time to get off your ass and get a little uncomfortable for a little while so you can live comfortably the rest of your life. A handful of your leads are good deals and you know it. Are you looking for them, or making excuses not to make contact? Somehow, you've got to muster up the guts to call these sellers and when you do, you'll discover:

- They need you more than you need them.
- They're easy to talk to and eagerly await your call.
- They'll do almost anything you ask most of the time.
- They're more afraid of you, than you are of them.

To get courage to excel you need cash flow. To get cash flow, you need deal flow. To get deal flow, you need to follow the five steps, fix what you break, quit whining about the small stuff, and get in the game. To get in the game and win it, you need all the training you can get, and quickly convert it to movement. A little bit of movement is better than a boatload of meditation.

Last year and this were extremely profitable years for our students who chose to play the game. The payoffs were huge, as evidenced by their letters; some are seen in this book, and the Wall Of Fame at Global Publishing is crowded.

I see a very bright next year for those with a little courage who want to be rich. It's a great time to be in the business. Don't waste it on mediocrity.

Welcome To The Family.
Dare To Be Great!

"All serious daring starts from within."

Harriet Beecher Stowe

If you'd like some free information on how you can get started as a real estate investor in your city go to: **www.RonsQuickStart.com**

Here's a photo of my grandson, Jesse... following in my footsteps!

I believe he has the courage to be rich!

"These classes are taught by people who have done what they teach and do it with expertise."
Dwane Stephens * Norco, CA

"This 4-day 'Quick Start' course is a thorough comprehensive seminar which provides the essentials to enable real estate investors to become transaction engineers. The presenting speakers are very competent, patient and pleasant to deal with. I highly recommend this training."
Brian N. Lee, M.D. * Los Angeles, CA

"Ron LeGrand is the absolute real deal. He is every bit of his tapes, CD's and books. The man is a walking wealth of information. I've never met anyone who is as knowledgeable in the real estate industry as Ron is. I would absolutely recommend anybody to go to the QTRES for well-grounded information in the real estate business." He is the bomb ("Boom Baby")
Thanks Ron
Michael L. Raysor * Newark, NJ

"This program was Amazing! Providing the A–Z of building a real estate business that can create massive wealth. I'm excited about the Masters Program and can't wait for the next training."
Eddie Twirling * Miami, FL

"I learned more in 4 days about making money in real estate than I've learned in the last 17 years as a landlord! I only knew about 2 ways to buy & sell before attending Ron's seminar. Now I know about 5+ additional ways to make money in real estate. Ron, where were you 17 years ago when I started??? I've never lost money in real estate. I wish I could say the same about the stock market."

Thanks to you and your team.
Linda Noriega-Wilson * Cranbury, NJ

Marilyn Williams

Dear Ron,

Here is my success letter of my first deal that I NETTED $61,000.00 in my Roth IRA!

I first heard about you on an infomercial late one night watching TV. I ordered your $69.00 introductory course. So when I told my husband about you he was very skeptical!

I then received information that you would be in Dallas, Texas at a one-day event promoting your program. My husband decided he at least needed to attend the event to hear what you had to say. We attended and purchased your three courses. He agreed to let me try the system and I followed your course step-by-step.

They first thing I did was to crank up the buying machine. I ran a daily ad in the newspaper. I also set-up with an answering service to take the calls following the script you have in your course.

I finally got the call I was looking for. A man called and said that he had purchased this house at a judicial sale. He was told that were liens and judgments against it. According to the information he provide there were. I then asked the magic question. **"Do You Want To Deed Me The House?"** He said yes he just wanted it out of his name. So I took the deed from your course and meet him and he signed it. I made him no promises telling him I would only record the deed if I could get clear title.

It ended up that the house was less than two years old and had never been completed by the contractor. Comps hon the house came in around $130,000.00 and it needed $20,000.00 to complete the construction. I based my asking price of $70,000.00 from the formula in your course.

I then opened title at a title company that I found that was willing to work with me. The title came back CLEAR! No liens or judgments!

Again, following your course I ran the "handyman Special" ad. I put a lock box on the house and gave the code out to the people that called from the ad. I had a full price contract on the house within a day! We closed two weeks later.

After back taxes and closing I netted $61,000.00 in my Roth IRA Tax Free For Life! I would say your system works!

Sincerely,

Marilyn Williams
Freedom Properties L.L.C.
Austin, TX 78759

"Everything at Ron's Quick Start Real Estate School was great! Don't change anything."
Richard J. Monnot - Laurys Station

"My name is Tom Black, a realtor® with a national brokerage. I have settled 44 transactions strictly as a realtor®. Had I known the techniques taught Nov 17-20 in Columbia, MD, I would have at least quadrupled my earnings. My partner and I are going to systemize our business. We are focused on generating $20-$50K in income over the next 90 days. The Less You Work, The More You Make is our NEW Mantra."
Tom Black - North East, MD

"This has been an incredible learning experience. Ron has taught me so much that I didn't realize I didn't know. After attending Ron's boot camp, I have complete confidence that I can go back to Albuquerque and start making the deals that will set my family up for a lifetime of success. I for-see myself making at least six figures within the next six months and have full intention of attending more seminars with Ron in Jacksonville in 2012. I would like to thank Ron and his staff a million times over for changing my life. However, a million still wouldn't cover it!"
Alice Hults - Albuquerque, NM

"Though I have made many false starts in real estate investing through various courses, my mind and actions have shifted, Ron's methods are the only ones that provide actionable steps. I feel confident I'll be a pro in a short time and leave the rat race. His

time proven system provides resources such as, legal forms, scripts, checklist matrixes, outside resources— services, websites, trainers. How to find services (Realtors®, attorneys). He delivers the live training with knowledge and humor.
Rachel Harris - Arlington, VA

"Ron - the master teacher! Good mix of information and opportunity!"
Claudia Tillery - Washington, DC

GLOSSARY

affidavit A written statement or declaration sworn to or affirmed before an authorized person.

agreement of sale A written agreement in which the purchaser agrees to buy and the seller agrees to sell. Terms and conditions are included in the agreement.

alienation clause Also known as a due-on-sale clause. This is a provision that allows a lender to demand payment of the balance of a loan in full if the collateral is sold.

amortization mortgage A debt for which the periodic repayments are used to reduce the principal outstanding as well as to pay off the current interest charges.

apportionment The adjustment of the income, expenses, or carrying charges of real estate that is usually computed to the date of closing of title so that the seller pays all expenses to that date. The buyer assumes all expenses from the date on which the deed is conveyed to the buyer.

appraisal An estimate of a property's value made by an appraiser who is usually presumed to be an expert in this work.

appraisal by comparison An estimate of value made by comparing the sale prices of other similar properties.

assignment The method or manner by which a right or contract is transferred from one person (the assignor) to another (the assignee).

assumption of mortgage This occurs when a person takes title to property and assumes the payment of an existing note or deed of trust.

balloon payment A final installment payment that pays off a debt.

beneficiary The person who receives or is to receive the benefits of a certain act.

bird dog/bird dogger A person who looks for houses that potentially fit the guidelines of the properties you prefer to purchase. Bird doggers will bring the information you require and you will reimburse them for their efforts on whatever basis you have agreed on.

bona fide In good faith; without fraud.

capital gain or loss The difference between the basis price (cost plus purchase expenses) of a capital asset and its sales price.

caveat emptor Let the buyer beware. The buyer must examine the goods or property and buy at his or her own risk.

chain of title A history of the conveyances and encumbrances affecting a land title from the time it was granted or as far back as records are available.

client The principal, the one who employs and compensates a broker.

closing date The date on which the buyer takes over a property.

cloud on the title An outstanding claim or encumbrance that, if valid, would affect or impair the owner's title.

codicil An addition to, or amendment of, a will.

collateral Additional security pledged for the payment of a debt. commission A fee charged for brokerage services.

commitment A pledge; a promise; an affirmation agreement.

complaint 1. In civil law, the initial statement of the facts on which a complaint is based. 2. In criminal law, the preliminary charge made against the accused.

comps See *appraisal by comparison.*

condemnation The acquisition of private property for public use with fair compensation to the owner. See also *eminent domain.*

conditional sales contract A contract for the sale of property stating that although delivery is to be made to the buyer, the title is to remain vested in the seller until the conditions of the contract have been fulfilled.

consideration Anything given as an inducement to enter into a contract, such as money or personal services. A contract, lease, obligation, or mortgage may subsequently be modified without consideration provided that the change is made in writing and signed.

contract A legally enforceable agreement.

covenants Agreements written into deeds and other instruments promising performance or nonperformance of certain acts or stipulating certain uses or restrictions on a property.

debt service Annual amount to be paid by a debtor for money borrowed.

deed An instrument in writing, duly executed and delivered, that conveys title to real
property.

deed restriction A restriction imposed in a deed to limit the use of the land. A deed might include clauses preventing the sale of liquor or defining the size, type, value, or placement of improvements.

default Failure to fulfill a duty or promise or to discharge an obligation; omission or failure to perform an act. In property foreclosure, usually the failure to pay loan installment
repayments when they become due.

defeasance clause The clause in a mortgage that permits the mortgagor to redeem his other property on payment of the obligations to the mortgagee.

defendant The party sued or called to answer in any lawsuit, civil or criminal.

deficiency judgment When the security for a loan is sold for less than the amount of the loan, the unpaid amount (the deficiency) is held by law (the judgment) to be the liability of the borrower unless the new owner has assumed the debt.

due-on-sale See *alienation clause.*

earnest money Down payment made by a purchaser of real estate as evidence of good faith.

easement A right that may be exercised by the public or individuals on, over, or through the property of others.

eminent domain A right of the government to acquire property for public use. The owner must be fairly compensated.

encroachment A building, part of a building, or obstruction that intrudes on the property of another.

encumbrance Any right to or interest in property interfering with its use or transfer or subjecting it to an obligation. In connection with foreclosure property, the most likely encumbrances are mortgages and claims for unpaid taxes.

equity In real estate, the difference between the value of a property and the amount owed on it. Also called the owner's interest.

equity loan Junior (subordinate) loan based on a percentage of the equity.

escrow A written agreement between two or more parties providing that certain instruments or property be entrusted to a third party to be delivered to a designated person upon the fulfillment or performance of some act or condition.

estate The degree, quantity, nature, and extent of interest (ownership) that a person has in real property.

estoppel certificate An instrument executed by the mortgagor setting forth the status of, and the balance due on, the mortgage as of the date of the execution of the certificate.

eviction A legal proceeding by a landlord to recover possession of real property.

exclusive agency An agreement to employ one broker only. If the sale is made by any other broker, both are entitled to commissions.

exclusive right to sell An agreement to give a broker the exclusive right to sell for a specified period. If a sale during the term of the agreement is made by the owner or by any other broker, the broker holding the exclusive right is, nevertheless, entitled to compensation.

executor A person or a corporate entity or any other type of organization named in a will to carry out its provisions.

fee (fee simple, fee absolute) The absolute ownership of real property. This type of estate gives the owner and his or her heir's unconditional power of disposition.

FHA Federal Housing Administration. See *FHA mortgage loan.*

FHA mortgage loan Mortgage loan insured by the Federal Housing Administration.

fiduciary A person who transacts business or handles money or property on behalf of another. The relationship implies great confidence and trust.

first mortgage Mortgage that has priority as a lien over all other mortgages. In cases of foreclosure, the first mortgage will be satisfied before other mortgages are paid off.

foreclosure A procedure whereby property pledged as security for a debt is sold to pay the debt in the event of default in payments or terms.

grace period Additional time allowed to perform an act or make a payment before a default occurs.

grantee The party to whom the title to real property is conveyed; the buyer.

grantor The person who conveys real estate by deed; the seller.

habendum clause The "to have and to hold" clause that defines or limits the quantity of the estate granted in the deed.

HUD Department of Housing and Urban Development. This agency has a broad mission in the entire housing industry. The specific area of interest to you, as an investor, is its involvement in subsidizing rents for low-income housing and the marketing of repossessed houses. Many of HUD repossessions provide excellent investment opportunities.

hypothecate To use something as security without giving up possession of it.

installments Parts of the same debt, payable at successive periods as agreed; payments made to reduce a mortgage.

intestate A person who dies before making a will or whose will is defective in form.

irrevocable Incapable of being recalled or revoked; unchangeable; unalterable.

joint tenancy Ownership of property by two or more persons, each of whom has an undivided interest with or without the right of survivorship.

judgment Decree of a court declaring that one individual is indebted to another and fixing the amount of such indebtedness.

junior mortgage A mortgage second in lien (subordinate) to a previous mortgage.

land contract In reality, a land contract is a promise to pay. In other words, if you buy a house under a land contract, you promise to pay an agreed-on amount on or before a specific date. Once the terms have been fulfilled, the seller will then deed the property to you.

landlord One who rents property to another.

land trust A means of taking control of a property anonymously. The only name that will appear on public records is the name of the trust and, usually, the name of the trustee. A land trust provides some asset protection in that it requires a good deal of digging via legal channels to discover if a person is the beneficiary of a trust.

lease A contract whereby for a consideration, usually termed *rent*, one who is entitled to the possession of real property, transfers such rights to another for life, for a term of years, or at will.

leasehold The interest given to a lessee of real estate by a lease. lessee A person to whom property is rented under a lease.

lessor One who rents property to another under a lease.

lien A legal right or claim on a specific property that attaches to the property until a debt is satisfied.

life estate The conveyance of title to property for the duration of the life of the grantee.

lis pendens A legal document filed in the office of the county clerk giving notice that an action or proceeding affecting the title to a property is pending in the courts.

LTV (loan-to-value ratio) Refers to the amount of money loaned on a property relative to its actual value. For example, a loan of $20,000 on a $40,000 house would have a 50 percent LTV.

marketable title A title that a court considers so free from defect that the court will enforce its acceptance by a purchaser.

mechanic's lien A claim made to secure the price of labor done on, and materials furnished for, uncompensated property improvement.

moratorium An emergency act by a legislative body to suspend the legal enforcement of contractual obligations.

mortgage An instrument in writing, duly executed and delivered, that creates a lien on real estate as security for the payment of a specified debt, which is usually in the form of a bond.

mortgage broker One who is paid to match borrowers with lenders.

mortgagee The party who lends money and takes a mortgage to secure payment.

mortgagor A person who borrows money and gives a mortgage on his or her property as security for the payment of the debt.

multiple listing An arrangement among members of a board of REALTORS® whereby brokers bring their listings to the attention of the other members. If a sale results, the commission is divided between the broker providing the listing and the broker making the sale.

non-qualifying assumption A mortgage or deed of trust that does not contain a due-on-sale clause, thereby allowing transfer of title freely without permission from the lender.

obsolescence Loss in value as a result of reduced desirability and usefulness of a structure because its design and construction have become obsolete.

open listing A listing given to any number of brokers with commissions payable only to the broker who secures the sale.

open mortgage A mortgage that has matured or is overdue and is therefore "open" to foreclosure at any time.

option A right given for a consideration to purchase or lease a property on specific terms within a specified time. If the right is not exercised, the option holder is not subject-to liability for damages. If exercised, the grantor of the option must perform.

payoff letter A letter from a lender stating the current balance due on an account; also referred to as an estoppel letter or certificate.

performance bond A bond used to guarantee the specific completion of an endeavor in accordance with a contract.

personal property Any property that is not real property.

plat book A public record containing maps of land showing the division into streets, blocks, and lots and indicating the measurements of the individual parcels.

points Discount charges imposed by lenders to raise the yields on their loans. One (1) point equals one percent (1%) of the loan amount

prepayment clause A clause in a mortgage that gives a mortgagor the privilege of paying the mortgage indebtedness before it becomes due, either with or without a prepayment penalty.

proration Allocation of closing costs and credits to buyers and sellers.

purchase money mortgage A mortgage given by a grantee or any other lender in partial payment of the purchase price of real estate.

quiet title suit A suit in court to ascertain the legal rights of an owner to a certain parcel of real property.

quitclaim deed A deed that simply conveys the grantor's rights or interest, if any, in real estate; generally considered inadequate except when interests are being passed from one spouse to the other.

real estate board An organization whose members consist primarily of real estate brokers and salespersons.

REO (real estate owned) Property acquired by a lender through foreclosure and held in inventory.

real estate syndicate A partnership formed for a real estate venture. Partners may be limited or unlimited in their liability.

real property Land and generally whatever is erected on or affixed thereto.

REALTOR® A term used to identify active members of the National Association of REALTORS® (NAR), This term is commonly used to refer to anyone licensed to sell real estate. However, the term *REALTOR®* applies only to dues-paying members of NAR.

recording The act of writing or entering, in a book of public record, instruments affecting the title to real property.

recourse The right to claim against an owner of a property or note.

red lining The refusal to lend money within a specific area for various reasons. This practice is illegal because it discriminates against creditworthy people who happen to live there.

release clause A clause found in a blanket mortgage that gives the owner of the property the privilege to pay off part of the debt and thus free part of the property from the mortgage.

repo A shortened or slang version of repossession, which occurs when a lender takes possession of the collateral that, was security for a loan.

right of redemption Right to recover property transferred by a mortgage or other lien by paying off the debt either before or after foreclosure; also called equity of redemption.

right of survivorship Right of the surviving joint owner to succeed to the interests of the deceased joint owner. This right is a distinguishing feature of a joint tenancy or tenancy by the entirety.

RTC (Resolution Trust Corporation) An organization set up by the federal government to market houses from the inventory of federally insured, defunct banks and other lending institutions.

sales contract A contract by which a buyer and seller agree to the terms of sale.

second mortgage A mortgage made by a homebuyer in addition to an existing first mortgage. The order of recording determines the seniority of the lien.

seller financing Refers to the owner of a property who agrees to carry a mortgage on the property that he or she is selling so that the buyer doesn't have to obtain any or all of the financing from another source or lending institution.

specific performance A remedy in a court of equity compelling a defendant to carry out the terms of an agreement or contract.

split funding A technique whereby an investor offers a small amount of cash to close a deal with the balance due at a later date in a form other than extended monthly payments.

statute of frauds Law requiring certain contracts to be made in writing or partially complied with in order to be legally enforceable.

subdivision A tract of land divided into lots or plots.

subordination See *subordination clause.*

subordination clause A clause in a mortgage that gives priority to a mortgage taken out at a later date. The seller agrees to go into a second, third, or fourth position allowing the buyer to obtain new financing senior to the seller's lien without paying off the lien from the proceeds.

substitution of collateral Taking an existing mortgage on one property and transferring it to another.

survey The process by which a parcel of land is measured and its area ascertained; also the blueprint showing the measurements, boundaries, and area.

tax sale Sale of real property after a period of nonpayment of real estate taxes.

tenancy at will A license to use or occupy lands and tenements (permanent and fixed property) at the will of the owner.

tenancy by the entirety An estate that exists only between husband and wife with equal right of possession and enjoyment during their joint lives and with the right of survivorship.

tenancy in common An ownership of realty by two or more persons, each of whom has an undivided interest without the right of survivorship.

testate Condition when a person dies leaving a valid will.

title company A firm that examines title to real estate and/or issues title insurance.

TPA (third-party administrator) One who is approved to administer funds from a retirement program. You must use a TPA to access money from your retirement accounts for self-directed activities.

without recourse Words used in endorsing a note or bill to denote that the future holder is not to look to the endorser in case of nonpayment.

wrap (wraparound loan) A new loan encompassing any existing loans.

Resources

Resources available through Ron's membership site, www.RonsGoldClub.com

By joining our elite community of real estate entrepreneurs from all over the country and Canada, you'll have the unique privilege and access to Ron's Forms and Agreements Library of over 500 attorney approved business letters, forms, notices and contracts listed below. You'll also have access to hundreds of training videos, Q&A sessions with Ron and an interactive forum to discuss deals with other investors and even ask Ron questions directly.

FORMS:

- ACTS Deal Checklist
- ACTS Lease Exhibit A
- Addendum for Possession After Closing
- Addendum for Possession After Closing – Canada
- Addendum to Option to Purchase Agreement
- Addendum to Real Property Possession and Lease Agreement Sweat Equity Program
- Affidavit and Memorandum of Agreement Concerning Real Estate
- Agreement and Declaration of Trust (Land Trust)
- Agreement and General Release
- Agreement for Assignment of Judgment
- Agreement for Deed – Buying
- Agreement for Deed – Selling
- Agreement for Purchase and Sale of Hotels
- Agreement for Purchase and Sale of Improved Real Estate
- Agreement for Purchase and Sale of Vacant Land
- Alberta Agreement For Sale – Canada
- Applicant Information Sheet
- Applicant Information Sheet – Canada
- Applicant Receipt Agreement
- Application Receipt Agreement – Canada
- Assignment
- Assignment of Beneficial Interest in Trust
- Assignment of Contract for Purchase and Sale
- Assignment of Rents and Leases
- Auction Template
- Authorization to Release Information
- Authorization to Release Information – Canada
- Buyer's Disclosure

- Cash Deal Checklist
- Certificate of Appointment of Successor Trustee
- Certificate of Resignation of Trustee
- Commercial Letter Of Intent
- Contingency Clauses
- Contractor Proposal Form and Work List
- Cost To Sell Worksheet
- Development and Profit Participation Agreement
- Disclosure Regarding Real Estate Transactions CYA
- Down Payment Addendum
- Down Payment Assistance Program
- Down Payment Assistance Program – Canada
- Escrow Agreement
- Escrow Letter
- Escrow Letter – Canada
- Executive Summary
- Exhibit C…
- Existing Note Worksheet
- General Release for Buyer When Closing Lease Option – ACTS Only
- General Release for Seller When Assigning Lease – ACTS Only
- Information Sheet with Comparables
- Instructions – Read Me First
- Investor Buyer Sheet
- Joint Venture Agreement for Assignment of Mortgage
- Land Installment Contract – Buying
- Land Installment Contract – Selling
- Lead Property Information Sheet
- Lease Option Agreement with Buyers
- Letter of Agreement and Addendum – CYA Purchase
- Letter of Agreement and Addendum – CYA Sale
- Limited Power of Attorney
- Limited Power of Attorney – Canada
- Loan Calculator with Balloon Payments
- Loan Closing Instructions
- Management Letter to Get Lender to Send You Notices and Payment Book
- Notice of Real Estate Option Agreement
- Notice of Substitution of Collateral – Canada
- Ontario Agreement For Sale – Canada
- Option To Purchase When Buying
- Owner Financing Deal Checklist
- Owner Occupant Buyers
- Owner Occupant Buyers – Canada
- PAM Chart
- Paper Trust Agreement
- Partial Release of Judgment
- Personal Property Trust Agreement
- Pro Forma – Operating Statement
- Program Questions and Answers
- Property Information Sheet – Mobile Homes and RV Parks

- Property Information Sheet – Multi-Family
- Property Information Sheet for Office Retail Space
- Property Information Sheet for Raw Land
- Property Inspection Summary
- Protection Clauses
- Radon Gas, Lead Paint and Mold Addendum
- Real Estate Purchase Option Agreement
- Real Property Possession and Lease Agreement Sweat Equity Program
- Release of Lien for Contractors
- Rental Contract
- Repair List
- Repairs and Inspection Agreement
- Security Agreement
- Seller's Acknowledgement (CYA)
- Short Form Lease Option Agreement with Sellers
- Short Form Lease Option Agreement with Sellers – Canada
- Short Sale Addendum (CYA)
- Standard Purchase and Sales Agreement
- Subject-To Deal Checklist
- Trust Agreement
- Warranty Deed to Trustee
- Your Game Plan
- Your Next Step
- Your Next Step – Canada

Join Ron's esteemed group of real estate entrepreneurs for a 30-day trial and get his **Wholesaling course for just $1** (Retail value $599) by going to **www.RonsDollarDeal.com.**

Download your electronic copy at: www.RonLeGrand.com/Resources

Lead/Property Information Sheet

Client/Student _____

Date _____   Owner's Name _____

Source _____   Cell Phone _____ Evening _____

Address _____   ★ Asking Price _____

City _____ State _____   ★ What do you think it would appraise for? _____

Area of town _____   Your comps _____ Rent comps _____
(Zesimate from Zillow)

Existing Mortgage Information (must have)

★
1st - $_____   Lender _____ _____ % Pmt _____

2nd - $_____   Lender _____ _____ % Pmt _____

Is Payment PITI ☐ Yes ☐ No   Current? ☐ Yes ☐ No   If NO – $_____ in Arrears

---

A

If asking price and loan balance are within $35,000:
Will you sell the house for what you owe on it?
★ Yes No *(circle one)*

↳ **If No** – If we take over your debt and pay all closing costs, what's the least you could accept for your equity? $_____

↳ **YES** – OK, I'll have my boss call to set an appointment. What's the best time?

B

If the house has a Mortgage and over $35,000 equity or A is a no:
If we can agree on a price and we accept all responsibility for future repairs would you consider a lease purchase? Yes No *(circle one)*

↳ **YES** – OK, I'll have my boss call to discuss terms. When is the best time? _____ *(get info below)*

↳ **NO** – So you're saying if you don't get full price and all cash you won't sell? Yes No *(circle one)*

↳ **YES** – OK, I understand but that wouldn't make sense for us. Thanks *(stop here)*

↳ **NO** – OK, I'll have my boss call to discuss several ways he can buy your home. What's the best time to call? _____ *(get info below)*

C

If the house is Free & Clear:
If Yes – Will you consider taking monthly payments for your equity? Yes No *(circle one)*

↳ **If No** – Would you consider a lease purchase making us responsible for all repairs? Yes No *(circle one)*

↳ **YES** – I'll have my boss call to discuss terms. When is the best time? _____ *(get info below)*

↳ **NO** – So you're saying if you don't get full price and all cash you won't sell? Yes No *(circle one)*

↳ **YES** – OK, I understand but that wouldn't make sense for us. Thanks *(stop here)*

↳ **NO** – OK, I'll have my boss call to discuss several ways he can buy your home. What's the best time to call? _____ *(get info below)*

How did you arrive at your asking price? _____ Reason for selling? _____

Does it need repairs? ☐ Yes ☐ No   Approximate amt $_____ ☐ Vacant ☐ Occupied

★ When do you want to move? _____   Is the house listed? ☐ Yes ☐ No

Down $_____
Month $_____
Term

Description:

★ Bed/Bath: _____   ★ Square Feet: _____   Lot Size: _____

Construction: Frame ☐   Brick ☐   Block ☐   Stucco ☐   Other_____

Garage: 0 1 2 Carport ☐   Basement ☐   Refrigerator ☐   Range ☐   Dishwasher ☐

★ Is it ☐ House   ☐ Condo?   Association fee $_____   ☐ Month   ☐ Year

Notes:_____
_____
_____
_____

Work less, make more and get you to the next level in your real estate investing business.

We've discovered the game-changing difference almost all six and seven-figure real estate investors have in common. This difference has proven critical in the level of their accomplishments for a few critical reasons. They have alleviated all the grunt work from their daily lives. They are focused on making important decisions and getting paid in the process. They pay a lot less each month for services because their business is stream-lined and runs on auto-pilot. They have more time to spend with loved ones. **They have Virtual Assistants!**

Virtual Assistants are fast becoming one of the most efficient and effective ways to get the critical help needed to run a successful real estate business. If you are serious about making more money, spending less of your personal time and truly want systemization then you need Gold Club Virtual Assistant Services.

Hiring a Gold Club Virtual Assistant allows you the luxury of focusing on your real job, which is making decisions that make you money. Our Gold Club VAs are all located here in our home office on Jacksonville, FL and trained daily. Gold Club VAs have all the systems in place and are highly skilled and dedicated staff to begin calling on sellers for you RIGHT AWAY! And, because they're not your employee, you won't have any of the costs associated with hiring, firing, payroll taxes, insurance, unproductive work or accounting.

Our focus is on delivering the best possible customer service, building and managing automated systems and ensuring you receive quality leads from our highly trained and skilled VA team, and this is our commitment to you. Our VAs have strong executive leadership and support who you'll also have direct access to communicate with for any reason and address any issues, concerns, and ask questions.

You'll also have direct access to your personal VA to communicate with by email and phone to ensure there are no delays in service and your expectations are met and exceeded.

Here's how it all works, our VA service comes with a Gold Club Membership, so you'll have access to all the resources you need in one place.

If you're done with mediocrity and truly want to propel your real estate business to the next level, call and get started with Gold Club VA services today. Just call **VIP Services at 888-840-8389** for all the details and to get your Gold Club VA team working for you today.

To order call
888-840-8389
EST 9am-5pm
Monday-Friday

Gold Club Membership Levels	$59 Gold Club Membership	$297 Gold Elite Membership	$697 Gold Elite VA Membership
Gold Club Membership Website			
Audio and video training, discussion areas, an ever-increasing number of tools and links, online application resources and more.	✔	✔	✔
Ron LeGrand's Lesson Videos			
Lesson videos on a variety of real estate topics, made available to members through the member website, Weekly Report and via E-mail.	✔	✔	✔
Live & Online Training Events			
Ron does frequent educational trainings on his own and with leaders throughout the industry on topics from real estate to online wealth building.	✔	✔	✔
Open Line Monthly Q&A			
You can fax your Property Information sheets to Ron on the second Monday of each month, then join him on the call where he will discuss your deals and answer your questions.	✔	✔	✔
The Gold Club Weekly Report			
Our Gold Club Weekly Report brings you the latest video from "Planet Ron," how-to articles and lesson videos to help you make the most of your training, an "Upcoming Events" calendar, "Ronisms," motivational quotes, Ask Ron video, contests and cartoons and humor submitted by Gold Club members.	✔	✔	✔
The Mentor Newsletter			
Every month you'll receive a special newsletter by mail (NOT EMAIL) that strives each month to teach, motivate, and always earn a place at the top of your "must-read NOW" pile, and A BONUS TRAINING CD at least 6 times per year.	✔	✔	✔
Database For Your Buyers & Sellers			
You will be set up with an email service to send your new properties to your buyers list.		✔	✔
DREAM Solutions Pro Buyer/Seller Website			
Interactive voice response system (IVR) to collect buyer information, Web Tools -built in Landing pages, Web Forms, Websites. Your Property Pipeline to manage all your current deals in one place. Marketing & Reporting tools to track your marketing efforts, Contact Management System for all your Buyers and Sellers (your email service and auto-response center, text blasts) Action center with your TO-DO list, message board to house and organize all your important messages.		✔	✔
Interactive Voice Response (IVR) System		✔	✔
FSBO Lead Service	✔	✔	✔
Virtual Assistants			
We'll hire, train, monitor and pay a VA to find and call FSBOs for you and deliver daily completed property information sheets with yes or no answers so you can spend your time calling only hot prospects. This should get you more leads than you can handle, but if you want more, say the word and you'll only be charged by the minute for overage. Your VA works for you with a dedicated phone line and email address for constant communication.	VA services may be purchased in 5 hour increments	VA services may be purchased in 5 hour increments	Includes VA services up to 25 hours

Free CD Order Form
of Ron LeGrand Interviews

As my way of saying thanks for buying this book I'd be pleased to send you any or all of the CDs below, each worth $19.95, **a total value of $79.80** for only $12.95 S&H. But there's a catch. Not a big catch, just a small favor. All I ask is you tell your friends about my book and maybe a polite nudge to get them to buy. My wife and kids would appreciate it.

Check the CDs you'd like:

❏ **How You Can Be A Quick Turn Real Estate Entrepreneur Without Previous Experience**
This frank discussion with Mentor Magazine explores the lucrative world of quick turn real estate and where the really big money is made including behind the scenes secrets rarely disclosed elsewhere.

❏ **Everything You Ever Wanted To Know About Land Trusts**
This interview answers every question ever asked about how, why and when to use land trusts to buy real estate and discusses the risks you take if you don't.

❏ **How To Sell Houses on Auto Pilot**
You'll see how this amazing ex-UPS employee buys and sells 5 to 10 houses each month and never talks to a buyer or shows a house.

❏ **How To Bomb Proof Your Assets**
This interview with a national attorney who specializes in asset protection, estate planning, tax reduction and entity structuring could save you a fortune and be the difference between keeping or losing a lifetime of wealth.

❏ **Where To Get The Money**
This interview explains where you can get all the money you'll need to buy and rehab properties regardless of your credit or financial condition. It contains the secrets banks don't want you to know and Ron explains how he got started with no money or credit and overcame bankruptcy to buy over 40 houses his first year.

Please Print Clearly
Name: _____ Spouse: _____

Address: _____

City: _____ State: _____ Zip: _____

Cell: (____) _____ Fax: (_____) _____

Email: _____

Please charge credit card _____, exp. date _____ $12.95 for S&H.

Authorized Signature _____

(Must have the information above. No PO Boxes please. S&H covers one or all CD's.)

Order online at **www.RonLeGrand.com/Resources**
Fax this completed order form to: **888-840-8385 or 904-262-1464** (24 hours/7 days a week)
Call 1-888-840-8389 (M-F 9am ET -5pm ET)
Mail this completed order form with check to:
Global Publishing, Inc. 9799 St. Augustine Road Jacksonville, FL 32257

Here's The Fastest And Easiest Ways To Make A Killing In Real Estate Today... Without Using Your Money Or Credit... And Build A Substantial 5-Figure Monthly Passive Income
By Ron LeGrand

Have you ever thought you'd like to buy and sell houses but didn't know how or where to get the money?

Are you so busy making a living you can't take time to make any real money?

Can you retire on what you have set aside, if any, and live comfortably while not depending on the government to be there if you need them?

If you don't like your answers, this report will show you how I extract over $50,000 a month from nice homes in beautiful neighborhoods needing no repairs and using none of my own money or credit.

What's more, I don't buy foreclosures, do short sales, renovate houses, borrow money, use my credit in any way, nor do I have a real estate license or any need to deal with banks, lenders or Realtors®...and I spend less than six hours a month running the entire business while owning several other businesses simultaneously.

Part Time Business – Full Time Income

You are about to see how my part-time business produces a very nice full-time income but more importantly to you it's a business you can enter with no previous experience and start profiting quickly...Earn while you learn...and all the automation and systemization you need is already set up for you so you hit the ground running…like thousands of my clients all over North America.

My name is Ron LeGrand and I'm the world's leading expert at quick turning houses. I'm in my 33rd year of buying and selling over 3,000 to date and still do 4-6 a month with a total staff of one personal assistant using part of her time for my real estate business. Googling me could keep you busy for hours. My story is at the end of this report if you care.

Let's get to what I do and how I can help you achieve a Quantum Leap.

But before I layout the business, I'll ask you to turn off your bullshit meter for a few minutes. I know you're skeptical and you should be. So am I. The whole world is full of crap and you can believe little of what you hear.

You can also believe I'm a tell-it-like-it-is guy, so in full disclosure, at the end of this report I'll be asking you to exchange a little of your money for a life changing education from a battle scared veteran of 33 years who makes millionaires all over the world. If that bothers you, this report isn't for you. It will be of no value.

OK, if you're still in, let's get started.

Most Common Profit Centers

In residential real estate, there are several ways to make money…The first two are…

1. Buy junkers and rehab them and sell to owner occupants who qualify for a new loan.

2. Flip these same junkers quickly to investors who want to rehab them and make a quick profit on houses you never own…we call this "Wholesaling."

Both of these methods require you to buy the house cheap, largely from banks and they'll all need minor or major rehab. If you **rehab**, you must raise the money to buy, have contractors, find qualified buyers and get them a loan several months after you buy. The average profit on these deals is from $20,000 to $40,000 nationwide and some make over $100,000 per deal.

Wholesaling means you simply make an offer through a Realtor® on a bank owned property at a deeply discounted price. When your offer is accepted, your Realtor® produces a contract for you to sign and you have 30 days to close. During that time, you locate a rehabber to flip your contract to for an average profit of $5,000 to $15,000.

You never own the house or have any costs. You just get a check for being the middle man/woman.

I get about one out of twelve offers accepted and never leave my desk to make them. I only visit the house after the offer is accepted and send the $1,000 deposit to the Realtor® if it's a go. Therefore, no risk until I know I want the house.

You see, I make offers from my iPad through a daily feed of houses from my Realtors®. The work has been removed from this business. I used to have to go look at a lot of houses to get one accepted. NO MORE! I buy two or three bank repos a month from my desk and wholesaling is one of the two fastest ways to get a check.

You'll need no credit, very little money, no repairs, short sales, bank loans, contractors or costly entanglements. You're in and out in less than 30 days without even owning the house.

I can and will teach you both wholesaling and retailing. I've done over 700 of each and likely the best qualified guy alive to do so. Certainly the best looking. (I'm Just Sayin')

So First, Let's Discuss The Easiest Way To Make Big Money

Let's talk about where the BIG EASY money is in real estate so you can see the whole picture. For every junker on the market today, there are over 25 pretty houses needing no work in all price ranges in every city in North America.

I just described the WHOLESALE AND RETAIL Business but there's another business within the business I call...

The PRETTY HOUSE Business

Within it, you'll find the fastest way to get a check but it also contains residual income and future revenue all from doing the job once.

Wholesaling and retailing have a huge drawback...

You Only Get One Check

If you don't keep working, you don't get paid.

I like to get paid whether I'm working or not. How about you?

If you want to replace your job or profession…and thousands of my clients have…the best way to do so is monthly revenue you can count on even if you're sick, on vacation or just don't want to work. Now add that to a one time check between $10,000 – $50,000 every time you do one of these deals…I do about 4 a month…and you can begin to see why any job is a waste of your time.

Stay with me. You promised to turn off your bullshit meter. It's all true and easy for me to prove, and yes, it applies to you and works in your city.

Never Use Your Own Credit

You will not apply for loans or ever use your own credit. That would be the largest mistake you could make. When you guarantee debt, you risk three things…your credit, your assets and your marriage. You'll never, ever apply for a loan on <u>Planet Ron</u>. No one will ever check your credit or ask for a financial statement.

So let's look at the Pretty House Business where your credit or your money will not be needed.

It's all about nice homes owned by owner occupants or FSBO's (For Sale By Owners).

But what makes the business so easy and fun is you'll never pay cash for these homes and sometimes you'll pay full market value and still make five figures within a few days.

The key is…

TERMS

We work with sellers who will sell with terms so we can offer terms to our buyers.

You see, 81% of people looking to buy a house can't qualify at a bank for various reasons. These become our prime pool of buyers because we can sell them a house on terms giving them time to fix what's broke in their lives and ultimately get bank financing. That could be credit, debt ratio, not enough down, self-employed, can't prove income yet or several other issues. All of which can be fixed with time.

A house becomes ten times easier to sell with terms than with cash, therefore we have the whole 81% to ourselves, while the Realtors® and builders fight over the 19%.

Some of that 81% have substantial down payments or option deposits measuring in the thousands and they will gladly give it to you to get a home of their own.

Many have had a home and lost it. Some are first or last time buyers. All have issues that can be fixed in a year or two. You are a blessing to them when you help them get in a home now and get their life and self-confidence back.

I've had buyers hug me with tears flowing, send me gifts, invite me over for dinner and openly thank God I came into their life. What we do is a huge public service, both to buyers and sellers.

By the way, everything is closed with attorneys…at the buyer's expense…with full disclosure in writing. No lies, deceit or shady practices are necessary or condoned by this old dog.

There are only two types of terms you will use to buy houses…

- You'll lease it with an option to buy and the right to sublease it with an option.

- You'll buy it with owner financing with the right to sell it any way you like. More on that in a minute.

Before I go any further, I know your skeptical brain is asking…

How Many Sellers Will Agree To TERMS?

Fair Question. Let me give you the answer.

It just so happens we have 16 virtual assistances at our company Global Publishing, whose job is to call sellers for our clients and collect info on their houses for sale. They find the sellers who advertise online in your city, call them for you, collect the facts and read a script to see if they would consider selling with terms…lease option or owner financing.

They make about 15,000 calls a month to the leads they generate and the leads you send them so we know the numbers well and here's the one that answers your question…

Out Of All The Sellers Our
VA's Reach On The Phone
36% Say "Yes" To Terms

You read that right. About a third of the FSBO's on the market will consider terms. This group comprises our entire Pretty House Business and we have no use for the rest, so they are quickly discarded.

It's easy for our inexpensive VA's to generate 10-15 leads a week for our clients. That means 3-5 sellers a week want to discuss terms. From those you can easily generate one deal netting you $10,000 minimum on the frontend and maybe some of that residual income I discussed earlier.

In the Pretty House Business, there are three main forms of income.

1. Non-refundable option deposits if you're selling with a lease purchase or a down payment if you're selling with owner financing. The minimum is $10,000 and you receive it 2-3 days after accepting your tenant buyer.

2. Many deals have a monthly spread between the rent or payment you receive and the payment you make. These can range from $200 – $3,000 per month on the luxury homes.

3. The backend profit, which is the difference between what your buyer owes you and what you owe the seller. This can be little or nothing or a substantial sum.

Our goal is to do deals that include all three income streams but sometimes we settle for only one, as you're about to see.

The numbers and the seller's needs will determine our profit centers. Virtual Assistants do 90% of the work and scripts help you do the rest.

Selling is even simpler because in the TERMS business there are only two ways to sell…

- You lease it to a tenant with the option to buy and collect several thousand dollars as a non-refundable deposit…which gets applied as their down payment when they get a loan to purchase. Once you collect the money, it's yours to keep whether they buy or not. You may use it immediately.

The tenant/buyer also agrees to pay the attorney fee and a monthly rent and a term of 1 – 3 years for them to get financed, plus they are responsible for all repairs.

- You sell with owner financing, collecting a down payment and a monthly payment until they get refinanced. You agree on a term going in and of course all responsibility of the house is theirs. The minimum down payment is $10,000 but most are higher depending on the value of the homes. The higher the value, the bigger the down.

> *"The More Dollars You Waller In*
> *The More Stick To You"*
> – Ron LeGrand

Let me display some case studies so you can get clear on what I mean. Here's a deal I did recently in Jacksonville, Florida where I live…

Market Value: $385,000

Loan Balance: $351,000

Payment: $1,925

The sellers were moving from this 3 year old house in two weeks and knew they couldn't make two house payments. The house was in excellent condition and payments were current. Upon first contact with our VA who collected the facts, the sellers said they'd sell the house for what they owed, which is actually very common.

Their main concern was debt relief. They'd had it listed and it didn't sell, so they needed an immediate exit strategy, which I knew I could provide after making a call to them. I made it clear I could buy their house with owner financing and make their payment until sometime in the future when it gets cashed out, but there's no way I'd pay off their loan now.

No TERMS – No Deal!

They agreed instantly and we executed a simple agreement on the spot. I asked for and received two months before the first payment was due so I had two months to locate a buyer I liked.

My goal from the beginning was to buy or control the house for the loan balance and then install a tenant/buyer to pay rent and in time get a new loan. That's exactly what happened.

After turning down several applicants because they didn't have a big enough option deposit to suit me, I finally found one in seven weeks with $50,000 down. I turned down several with $10,000 to $25,000 down, knowing the house would bring more.

Here's the numbers...

Sales Price: $395,000
Non-refundable option deposit: $50,000
Rent to me: $2,500
Term: 2 years

It was a family with good income, both working and their credit was near a score good enough to get a loan but maybe six months away. They are working with a good credit repair company and will be ready soon.

Frankly, I'm in no hurry. Here's why!

I made...

- $50,000 cash the day they leased the house

- $525 per month until they buy it

- ($2,500 rent minus $1,925 payment)

The longer this Golden Goose stays alive, the better I like it.

FYI, the tenant buyers are responsible for 100% of any repairs needed. It's a condition of all my options and has been for 30 years.

So let's see...I netted $50,000 in 2 months and $525 a month for two years or so with...

• No credit • No money
• No banks • No Realtors®
• No repairs • No loans
• No short sales • No costly entanglements

How many of these deals would you need to surpass your current income? My friend, I can have you doing one a month part-time within 90 days if you say yes to my offer at the end of this report. I won't promise you fifty grand but I will say $10,000 is our bare minimum and we get that on $125,000 houses.

By the way, if my tenant buyer doesn't buy and moves, their deposit is non-refundable. They won't get it back and they wouldn't expect to.

About half do move and forfeit their deposits when smaller amounts from $10,000 to $25,000 are accepted. I'm sure this couple will buy.

But, there's other ways to profit in this Pretty House Business and this report won't cover all of them.

Here's a simple deal my client Kirsti from Oregon did recently…

A seller agreed to lease option a house to her at $699,000 with a $7,000 deposit and a $7,000 monthly rent. That's every dime the house was worth and Kirsti knew it. However, I trained her how to profit with no risk, so here's what she did.

She clearly explained to the seller using my script that she would agree to her terms but would need to locate a tenant buyer she liked before the agreement would begin.

In other words, the seller knew if Kirsti didn't find a buyer, there would be no deal or $7,000 deposit from Kirsti. Nor would Kirsti ever pay a $7,000 rent out of pocket.

No Risk To Kirsti

Once this agreement was signed with this clear understanding, Kirsti ran some free online ads to find a buyer. The key words in the ad were…"Lease Purchase," No Bank Qualifying."

A tenant buyer came along with $50,000 down and agreed to a 3 year lease purchase at $744,000 at $7,000 a month.

Since there was no reason for Kirsti to remain in the deal, she simply assigned her agreement with the buyer to the seller and exited…with her

$42,000 Net Profit

…on a house she never owned or laid a finger on.
This type of deal is called ACTS, (Assignment of Contracts and Terms System).

I created ACTS about 3 years ago and it has made a lot of students a lot of money, even on over leveraged houses.

Let me point out…

- The seller got full price with no commission, even though it will take a while to cash out. This was her decision. In the meantime, she collects $7,000 a month with no repair responsibility.

- The buyer got a beautiful house with instant access and three years to qualify for a loan and the value to increase.

- Kirsti got $42,000 for what she knows, not from what she invested.

My Pretty House TERMS Cash Flow system contains everything she needed to pull off this deal, including forms, agreements and scripts for every type of seller and buyer.

I could go on for days with examples of deals, including multi-million dollar houses with six figure paychecks without risk...but at this point, I think you've read enough to see this business is worth your time to investigate and my brand new TERMS system will answer your questions and fill in the blanks.

Before I describe it, I'll make a bold statement to you that I truly believe and will back up.

The Decision You Make Here
May Be The Most Important
Financial Decision Of Your Life

You see, I built this system over years of trial and error and work with students nationwide to implement it. I see the results. I know its value.

Please consider my offer carefully. It may change the way you think about money, how to make it, how to keep and grow it and your current and future lifestyle.

It's Hot Off The Press

Recently, I recorded a two day seminar called TERMS. I went through the entire business from beginning to end in a laymen's step-by-step process.

Part of the training was to actually process deals the students brought to class. We called them in class, got orally accepted terms and completed the appropriate agreements for the students to go home and get signed. We even scheduled the appointment for them.
All of this was filmed and there are two DVD's in your system with live deal structuring. There was a lot of money generated for these lucky folks.

After the event I recorded several calls I made to sellers on the two CD's and included them. You'll see how I get them to make me an offer by reading my own scripts and asking them the key questions.

We Don't Make Offers
We Ask Questions And Let The
Seller
Make Us Offers

Of course all scripts are included, even one to set an appointment and another if they say no to terms. You see...

When Using My Script About
1/3rd Of The Sellers Who Say
"No" To Terms Turn Into A "Yes"

There's another two CDs with questions and answers along with the eight CDs and DVDs of the training.

Here's some of the things I covered in this new TERMS System.

With my **Pretty House Cash Flow System** you'll learn how to get ownership of beautiful homes in neighborhoods you'll be proud to be in. The system includes:

- How to work with higher priced houses and totally avoid risk or the fear of making monthly payments you can't afford. The higher the price the higher the profit.

- A **step-by-step start up plan designed for beginners** who've never bought a house in their life.

- There are two CDs in this system where I interview real sellers and you get to hear both sides of the conversation. You'll tune in while I pre-screen the sellers and when I hang up I discuss whether I would go see the house or not. If it's a go, I cover what kind of offers I'd make based on what the seller told me. If they pass my pre-screening test, I'll go see the house. If not, why bother? The real art is in the pre-screening and knowing what to ask. It's a 20-year craft I've perfected loaded with magic words that get results. You'll get it all, complete with proven tested scripts to follow. You don't need to create or write anything. I've done it all for you. Just follow each step I've laid out and watch it work. It's literally dot-to-dot.

- How to use land contracts and wrap-around mortgages to buy and sell and why they should be in every real estate entrepreneur's toolbox.

- **Ten things that tell you it's a deal...before you even see the house!**

- **How to create solutions for houses with little or no equity that are financed sometimes even over 100%, and <u>create tremendous profit</u> centers for you while getting the seller out of a home nobody else can buy.**

- How to eliminate banks from your life forever so you'll never be at the mercy of a loan committee.

- How to create the most flexible financing there is with no banks or personal liability and create tremendous income streams for you.

- How to set up immediate income, monthly cash flow, and a final payday all from the same deal.

- This is how to get out of your job or low paying business. The frontend checks are great but I'll work with you to create a monthly residual income from your current income. Then when you step down, you're covered even if you don't like working. That's true financial freedom.

- **Low-cost marketing techniques to attract motivated sellers to call you and pre-screening tools so you only deal with the most motivated of the batch. And how to pre-screen them in less than two minutes.**

- The secret question to ask every seller to get to their bottom line price instantly.

- How to structure your sale to <u>**create enormous incoming payments and cash flow**</u> and eliminate defaults and risks.

- How to attract dozens of motivated buyers who can't qualify at the bank, but are excellent prospects for your no qualifying financing.

- The most common mistakes for all investors to avoid when buying and selling.

- Looking for a home for your family? Most of my students find their dream home while doing deals. Remember, the first example I showed you on the $395,000 house? I didn't have to sell it. I could have moved in with no money out of pocket, no credit, no personal guarantee, no qualifying, no banks, no committees and no delay. Some do.

- How to find and acquire your next residence in a lovely area without using bank loans, credit or down payments.

- How to take control and start the cash flow with no risk or investment and make huge profits on nice houses even when you pay almost full retail price.

- How to **profit from any house**, regardless of the underlying financing.

- How to control lovely homes in beautiful neighborhoods in any market in North America without ever owning them, buying them, borrowing money, or incurring risk.

- How to solve sellers' problems when Realtors®, attorneys, and other real estate investors don't have a clue.

- **Why properties sometimes financed at 90 to 120% are your absolute best deals and give you the best paydays.**

- How to handle and overcome all common seller objections.

- How to build credibility and confidence with your seller from day one even if you're new.

- How to make sure you won't have to make a monthly payment out of your pocket and never worry about risk again.

In each of these systems, I spend many hours teaching you every aspect of this diverse, yet relatively simple business. There are dozens of word for word scripts so you'll never have to wonder what to say.

Easy To Sell

One of the common things people fear about getting into real estate investing is they're afraid they can't sell the house and somehow they'll get stuck with it. I can understand why this would create anxiety for a beginner because they simply don't have enough facts to overcome the fear. But the truth is…

Selling Houses Should Be the Easiest Part of Your Business, and I'll Show You How To Do It At Lightning Speed.

In an easy market it doesn't take a brain surgeon to sell a house, but in a slow hard market it takes a unique selling proposition to move a property fast and furious. We have one. It's called TERMS.

Here's What You'll Learn About Selling Houses Fast In Any Market...

- How to set the house up to show itself with no human intervention so you'll never have to risk your life and waste your time meeting prospects.

- How to match the house to the buyer and quit looking for perfect prospects.

- Why cashing out immediately is the most costly exit you could pick and cuts your profits in half, and how to fix it and still have a huge cash flow.

- I'll hand you guerrilla marketing techniques you can use on a paupers budget to drive in a herd of buyers within 2 days. Your entire cost to sell a house should be less than two hundred dollars.

- How to capture all incoming calls and never talk to anyone until they've seen the house, fall in love with it, have been instructed how to buy and what to do next, filled out an application and submitted it to you on a website we will provide and get set up for you in 5 days.

- The fastest, cheapest and best methods to find buyers in order of value – They're all free.

- What signs are the most effective and why mine get three times the results of others.

- How to get all kinds of cool stuff free as part of the buyers down payment to you. A free Harley is better than one you pay for and your wife will love you for all the new jewelry she'll get that you'll never have to buy. How about a boat or RV? I and some of my students get a lot of free stuff as part of their down payment on houses we get with no cash out of pocket.

This is the best, most up-to-date information ever put together to teach you exactly how to sell a house in any market. I'd remind you we are selling with TERMS to 81% of the market. A house is 10 times easier to sell on terms than to qualified buyers. Our buyers qualify if they have the money, not credit, and that money changes hands a few days after we accept them.

You Are The Loan Committee

You and you alone, decide and I'll show you how to do exactly that and turn you on to our source that does all the screening for you after you find your best prospect. It's the same source that will work with your buyers to clean up their credit and get them financed later.

My source will tell you when and if he can get them a loan, check their credit, background, criminal search and even compute their debt ratio, Your decision will be easy and my marketing system will provide you with multiple prospects to choose from.

When You Make A House Easy
To Buy It Becomes Easy To Sell

Your buyers list is built automatically for you, so as your prospects call or go online, the pertinent information is collected, mainly how much they have to put down, and stored in your database we provide.

If you wish, we'll even provide a VA (Virtual Assistant) to retrieve the information off your automated voice mail system that collects the information and call the buyers for you that have money and send them to the house, then follow up after.

This Information is Priceless When You Consider You'll Be Selling Houses As Fast As You Can Buy Them! And 90% of the work is done by our Virtual Assistants.

Don't worry, if your objective is to cash out quickly and find mortgage ready buyers, I've got that covered in my <u>Wholesale and Retail Cash Flow System</u> which I'll describe in a minute.

But first, let's finish the discussion of my new system that's already fast becoming an industry standard across North America.

But I'm not done yet...You'll also learn:

- How to handle the taxes and insurance and who should collect them and why. It isn't you.

- When you should never put someone in your house.

- How to make your buyers the best source of buyers for your next house. Most of my houses are sold to friends or relatives of previous buyers.

- How to get a financial commitment from a prescreened buyer without taking your house off the market. A special agreement I use will allow you to process five buyers on one house with no commitment to any of them. You get to pick and choose the best. If I'd had this agreement 20 years ago it would have saved me a lot of grief.

- The 6 steps to getting your buyer to the closing table whether you're selling with lease purchase or owner financing.

Stupid mistakes to avoid when selling houses. Each one probably cost me six figures to learn.

Wouldn't it be cool if you could buy 2 or 3 houses a month and never get involved in the sales process and know your product is moving as fast as you can buy it?

My 33 years of Quick-Turning properties of all shapes and sizes, in all neighborhoods, with all kinds of financing and finagling, with all sorts of sellers and competing against all sorts of would-be investors and professionals, deals done with lots of cash to spare and some with very little spare cash to spend, deals in the winter, spring, summer, and fall, in good times and bad, in buyers' markets and in sellers' markets, all of this…over 3,000 deals in all, have given me insight in to what constitutes a complete deal from start-to-finish, and the absolute ability to convey to you more than just a grab-bag of techniques.

The Pretty House Business
But There's Also The Wholesale and Retail Business

In my WHOLESALE AND RETAIL CASH-FLOW SYSTEM you'll get my complete system for making fast cash from single-family houses in the wholesale and retail business. You'll get step-by-step instructions on…

- How to create a $10,000 paycheck within the first 30 days in business without ever owning a house.

- How to eliminate risk and the need for operating capital while creating a $10,000 a month income without tenants.
- How to pre-screen callers so you can deal with only the cream of the crop. All of the scripts are included.
- How to make sure your repair costs never exceed your estimates (This one discussion could pay for the whole course!) This is assuming you want to do repairs, you certainly don't have to.
- How to have a house completely rehabbed in less than two weeks, no matter how bad the condition.
- **How to make money without ever talking to or meeting with a seller face-to-face.**
- How to determine true market value of a single-family house without hiring appraisers.
- **A step-by-step guide through the art of making an offer on a single-family house. It took me ten years to perfect this simple system that prevents failure and keeps you from making mistakes. This one part of the manual alone is worth the entire cost.**
- How to attract a long list of cash customers eager to buy your junkers, fix them up and sell them for a profit.
- Four simple questions to ask each potential buyer so you can build a list of people ready to snap up every property you have.
- **Complete agreements you can use in any state and an entire CD of instructions. You'll be using this every time you actually take ownership of a property to protect your privacy and keep away the predators.**

- Why you never have to do manual labor fixing up plumbing, paint, or repairs on a run-down single-family house and still make $10,000 a month.
- One entire CD dedicated to how to find and pre-screen a real estate agent to put on your team while they're pre-screening you.
- A guided tour of every component of a house, deciding what should be fixed and how much it should cost to repair.
- Another CD explains how to get all the money you need to buy and fix houses regardless of your personal qualifications. You'll never use credit or banks and the supply is endless. Of course it only applies if you want to buy and rehab. Wholesaling houses for a quick $10,000 doesn't require capital, you never buy the house.

By the way, the minimum profit I'll allow any of my students to make on a retail deal is $30,000. That's after all expenses are deducted. And that's the minimum, not the average. If you can't make $30,000 or more, I can assure you the problem is you. Some little piece was left out. My checklist will prevent those expensive little pieces from costing you money.

You'll also learn how to make your buyers the best source of buyers for your next house. Most of my houses are sold to friends or relatives of previous buyers.

Then we'll discuss how to get Realtors® to sell the house for you without you taking all the risk. I'll show you an easy system to make your house a priority for them so they focus on getting it sold, rather than all the others in their system.

I've let Realtors® sell houses for me on numerous occasions in the past and my system made it smooth as silk.

How to build a buyers list fast of wholesale buyers for quick flips and qualified retail buyers if you want to rehab and sell. This only takes about a month and will continue to grow automatically so soon you'll be...

Finding Houses For Buyers, Not Buyers For Houses

Imagine a business where buyers are waiting for your product so selling is a non-issue. The demand outweighs the supply so you can focus on buying.

OK Ron, How Much?

My entire system, which includes Pretty House TERMS Cash Flow and Wholesale and Retail Cash Flow Systems, a complete education in all the fastest and easiest to make money in real estate, at a total cost of just $2,497.

Wow Ron, That's A Lot Of Money!

You might think $2,497 is a lot of money to spend for training materials, but let's analyze it for a moment. The truth is you'll spend that much whether you purchase my system or not. You see, there are really only three choices.

Your First Choice is to throw this letter away and do nothing. That's the path of least resistance which many people take. And it's why so many of them are broke. If you never launch your ship, it'll never come back loaded with gold. By doing nothing, you'll pay for my system many times over in lost income.

Your Second Choice is to try it on your own, without proper training. I know from experience you'll make mistakes, and they'll cost you many times the price of my system. It's nearly impossible to avoid them! The "School of Hard Knocks" is the most expensive tuition you can possibly pay and your chances of success is slim.

It's Impossible To Learn What I Know Cheaper Than What I Charge.

By not using my scripts alone it'll cost you more than what I'm asking on your very next deal because you don't say the right things. How quickly could you exceed $2,497? In a heartbeat! If a lack of training makes you offer too much for a house, the difference will be in the thousands. What if you miss out on a single deal because you didn't know where to look, how to pre-screen or what to offer? Your loss will make my course cost seem miniscule.

Even if you only learn how to buy your next home for your family by eliminating banks, credit and down payments, that alone will be worth your investment. But, I assure you, you'll get a lot more than that. In fact, you'll get far more than $2,497 in value by the time you get through the first CD, plus I'll even finance it for you.

You'll Pay For My System Many Times Over If You Don't Order Them.

Your Third Choice is to order the entire Pretty House Cash-Flow Terms System today, and put the tools I give you to work. When you make that choice, not only will the cost become insignificant, you'll be getting a huge payback – all because you chose to take action. If you'll do your part, we'll do ours. Pick up the phone and call right now 800-567-6128, you have everything to gain.

Yes, I know there are dozens of real estate courses on the market a lot cheaper than $2,497. Most of them are good stuff; some are junk. Most of today's teachers were trained by me.

I don't have anything bad to say about any of my so-called competitors. Some are friends of mine. They're all real people and some actually buy a house now and then.

To be honest, if all you care about is saving a few bucks, it might be best you take the cheap seat first, and then come to me. I owe my competitors a debt of gratitude. They spend a fortune finding people who are interested in real estate and ultimately most make their way to me before it's over. Why? It's simple. My stuff really works. I'm truly making millionaires.

There Is No One Out There Like Me, I'm The Best In The World At What I Do (quite modest too)

You're not buying a course, it's a complete system. You're buying into a family of movers and shakers all over the country that faced the same decision at one time you're facing now…to pass or play.

If you honestly believe you'll get a million dollar education for $179, buy their stuff. It'll look pretty on your shelf. At least you saved some money.

If you want to get filthy, stinking rich with a proven system that's thirty years in the making and has thousands of success stories…Come to Papa.

Yes, it costs a little more but you'll understand why when you get it. Gosh, they come with over 24 CDs and a 6 DVDs and systems manuals full of forms, scripts, objections and steps a layman can follow, daily support by phone and email, some bonuses and a challenge I'll discuss in a minute, and of course no risk.

Here's Another $1,997 <u>In Free Bonuses</u> For Ordering Now:

Bonus # 1 – $1,000 Rebate Certificate
It's simple. Go do a terms deal that nets you $5,000 or

more within 90 days and prove it to me and I'll send you a check for $1,000. There's no catch. I will use your testimonial but you'll get a check. It's simply my way of challenging you to use the valuable information you're about to receive. We will be writing a lot of checks and happy to do so.

By the way, if you get to Jacksonville, stop by the office. You'll see 53 employees working every day to serve your needs and on every wall hangs testimonial letters with copies of checks and raving fans. I hope you'll be on our wall soon.

Bonus #2 – 90 Day Phone And Email Support
You may call or email all your questions to our trained consultant five days a week. He'll help you through deals and be by your side from the beginning to end. It's his job and you'll have no trouble getting him on the phone. All calls and emails will be answered same day. I want you to have a qualified advisor by your side so you're never

alone. This service sells separately for $497 for 90 days. It's free with your order.

Bonus #3 – $500 Discount

As a brand new student deduct $500, making your cost only $1,997.

My math says that's $1,997 in real value, plus my new system you'll get, if you order now.

But just to make you feel at ease, here's my unconditional guarantee...

Guarantee

Accept my offer and you have 30 days to return my Cash Flow Systems for a 100% refund, if for any reason you don't feel it's for you. No reason needed, no questions asked.

There Is Absolutely No Risk

Well, I've made my case the best I know how. At this point you're, either in or out. My life will pretty much go on the same regardless of your decision. How about yours?

Look, this isn't a life threatening choice. No one will die. Frankly it's just a small decision among many you've made today. I doubt the $1,997 will strain your budget, and I know it won't make a major impact on mine.

I'm making millionaires all over America and I'll continue to do it with you or without you. I learned a long time ago...only when the student is ready can the teacher appear.

Tax Deductible...Oh, did I forget to mention?

This system is tax deductible if this is your business. That means our good ole' Uncle Sam, is willing to pay about a third of your investment. Check with your accountant on this, but what it comes down to is a 28% – 35% discount in tax savings since it's a business expense. Ain't that neat?

So, Let's recap...

You get...

- My new Pretty House TERMS $1,497
- Wholesale and Retail System $1,000
- 90 Day support $497
- $1,000 Rebate Certificate $1,000
- A $500 Discount $500

Total Real Value $4,494
All for only $1,997

You are under no obligation to take me up on this offer, but be warned. You'll not see this offer anywhere else ever again. I honestly believe I've just offered you a proven way anyone can earn big bucks in the real estate business...and I guarantee it.

But remember, this is a one-time offer, and you MUST take advantage of this opportunity now as it will not be presented to you again at this price. The $500 discount is only available within your first 30 days as a new student.

To order, call 800-567-6128 and tell them to give you "Ron's new student discount from his book."

To Your $uccess,
Ron LeGrand

P.S. There are undoubtedly things you want to do that your current job or business can't provide. Maybe it embarrasses you or frustrates you to say "we can't afford it" to your spouse and family. Maybe you secretly lose sleep worrying about not getting ahead year after year. What would you do with an extra $100,000 – $250,000 this year? And every year?

- Would you pay off bills and make your family debt-free? Would you remodel the house, new kitchen, new carpet? Buy a new car, boat, even a second vacation home on the lake or in the mountains?
- Set aside all the money for the kids' college? Retire early? Help a family member in crisis?
- Yes, I know the very idea of having an extra $100,000 to $250,000 a year sounds ridiculous, especially given my promise of needing no money or credit. But, my friend, it is very real and given the chance, I'll prove it.
- Look, you're not going to get a $100,000 raise from your boss or your business. So, where else could you possibly get this kind of pay increase?
- The answer is nowhere, except PAPA.
- What if I'm right? What if everything I've said here is true and you pass up the opportunity? I can assure you every word is true. Read the enclosed testimonials. Real people! Give me a chance to help you become one of them.

- Forget about the cost and think about the value. Think about your family who depend on you to make the right decisions. Say yes before the window closes. I promise you'll be glad you did.

"The courses I purchased have really changed my life. I no longer work to pay someone else's bills. So far in two months, I've worked just about every deal explained in your courses, and my income has skyrocketed! Your courses are very thorough and self-explanatory leaving little to the imagination. I just want to thank you Ron for putting together such a dynamic course."

~ Bill Milligan, Vancouver, WA

To order call
800-567-6128
EST 9am-5pm
Monday-Friday

Or go to:
www.RonLeGrand.com/CFS